THE POLITICS AND ETHICS OF EVALUATION

The Politics and Ethics of Evaluation

Edited by
CLEM ADELMAN

CROOM HELM
London & Canberra
ST. MARTIN'S PRESS
New York

© 1984 C. Adelman
Croom Helm Ltd, Provident House, Burrell Row,
Beckenham, Kent BR3 1AT
Croom Helm Australia Pty Ltd, 28 Kembla St.,
Fyshwick, ACT 2609, Australia

British Library Cataloguing in Publication Data

The Politics and ethics of evaluation.
   1. Curriculum evaluation
   I. Adelman, Clem
   375'.006   LB1570

   ISBN 0-7099-0534-3

All rights reserved. For information, write:
St. Martin's Press, Inc., 175 Fifth Avenue, New York, NY 10010
First published in the United States of America in 1984

Library of Congress Cataloging in Publication Data
Main entry under title:

The politics and ethics of evaluation.

   Includes bibliographical references and index.
   1. Universities and colleges – United States – Administration – Evaluation – Addresses, essays, lectures.
2. Universities and colleges – United States – Curricula –
Evaluation – Addresses, essays, lectures. 3. Examinations
– United States – Validity – Addresses, essays, lectures.
4. Educational surveys – United States – Addresses, essays,
lectures. 4. Educational surveys – United States – Addresses, essays, lectures. I. Adelman, Clem.
  LB2341.P623   1984   379.1'54   83-40173

   ISBN 0-312-62619-3

Printed and bound in Great Britain

CONTENTS

Acknowledgements

Acknowledgements

The editor would like to thank Professors Brian Simon, Jim Eggleston and David Jenkins; Stephen Sedley, Q.C., Heather Lyons and David Smetherham for contributing to the various seminars at which versions of these chapters were first presented. Professor Harold Berlak's timely intervention helped to improve the Introduction.

THE POLITICS AND ETHICS OF EVALUATION

INTRODUCTION

Clem Adelman

In the past twenty years, evaluation endeavours have extended beyond localised assessment of student learning and the efficacy of curriculum design into education systems, nationwide programmes of development and into policy. Evaluators, without recourse to precedents, have been singed by political issues contested in the public realm. In this book evaluators reflect on the ways in which they have coped with the contradictions between their methodological precepts and the consequences of their actions and reports.

The worth of evaluation and the ethics of its procedures had, by the late 1950's, become sources of contention in the context of efforts to develop co-operative school/university programmes of curriculum development,[1] particularly those based on institutions in the Boston area of the U.S.A. The majority of the sources required to reconstruct those debates remain unpublished, yet a full account of the accumulated experience would have to deal with those problems of evaluation and curriculum development. Those debates were first drawn together in a publication "Perspectives on Curriculum Evaluation" (Stake, 1967) part of a series under the aegis of the American Educational Research Association. The stipulation that evaluation be linked to all programmes of educational development funded under the Title I Act[2] (1965) had given evaulation enhanced public attention. Through evaluation the productivity of an educational programme was to be appraised and any further grants to a programme being made conditional on information from such evaluation. In some cases consideration of the evaluation report lead to termination of funding. Most of those who worked as evaluators for those programmes had been trained in psychometrics and experimental design and used these methods in the course of evaluation. Their reports were subject to criticism by programme developers for lack of appreciation of educational issues, and by those responsible for making decisions about further funding, for overlooking criteria upon which the productivity of the programme might be judged. Some evaluators were sensitive to these problems of external validity - the case of curriculum development and evaluation in Boston has already been mentioned. These debates were subsequently amplified by leading

1

figures in the field of educational measurement such as Ralph Tyler, Michael Scriven and Robert Stake who began to question the wisdom of using methods modelled on psychometrics and experimental design for the purposes of evaluation.

At the meetings of the American Educational Research Association from about 1962, the assumption that evaluation was part of educational testing was disputed. With the publication of the AERA monograph series, evaluation became defined as a legitimate area of public debate. Tyler, Stake and Scriven were concerned that evaluation should not be seen by grant-makers, practitioners of evaluation and their students as a variant of educational testing. That and subsequent monographs, although mainly addressing problems of methodology and technique, also began to clarify the responsibilities of the evaluator in relation to the curriculum developers and to the grant-making agencies.

These ethical relationships are embodied in the methodological distinction made by Scriven (1967) - that of summative and formative evaluation. That distinction drew attention to the consequences of when and to whom the evaluation report might be released. In the summative type the evaluator releases the report at the end of the enquiry, whilst in the formative, reports are prepared and released as the programme develops, informing the developer and others who are given access to these reports. The formative, summative distinction poses questions of who should have rights of access to these reports and how the formative evaluation might respond to reactions from curriculum developers, those in the funding agencies, in the community in which the programme was developed and implemented and the institutions and individuals involved. Instead of a technical accomplishment, evaluation began to be seen as raising ethical, political and for those with a background in measurement and testing, "new" methodological problems. Even ardent measurement people like Popham (1975) warned students of evaluation:

> "Education evaluators must realise that their expertise is no substitute for tactful interaction with those around them. Evaluators who walk into an educational setting and expect deferential treatment merely because they know omega squared, are in for a surprise".

Under the rebrics of "Responsive evaluation" (Stake, 1974), "Democratic Evaluation" (McDonald, 1974) and "Transactional Evaluation" (Rippey, 1973), the implications of giving subjects rights to designate the topics of enquiry (reponsive evaluation) the "right to know" (democratic evaluation) and to enhance participants mutual understanding of the process of change, (transactional evaluation), are elaborated. These evaluative approaches intend to encourage participation by using forms of expression that are comprehensible to a wider range of audiences. Earlier evaluative reporting was expressed in forms that were just as specialist as those used in psychometrics or social anthropology. One favoured means of reporting is the case study (Walker, 1974). The richness of detail of both context and action, make case study as a methodology and a form of reporting suitable for evaluators who seek to address a wide audience and who wish to have their work acknowledged as authentic, accurate and fair by all parties that the case study addresses. However, case study used in evaluation is not merely a means of reporting but raises very sharply those central issues of access and confidentiality. As Walker (1974) states:

> "For the case study worker confidentiality does represent a continuous rather than an intermittent concern. It is not simply a question of negotiating access to the field at the start of the research and publication at the end . . . At every stage of the research and with almost every encounter the case study worker must continually monitor what he says in order not to breach the confidentiality given to other participants."

Methodology in the social world is about the procedures selected, devised and used for regulating relations between the evaluator and the subjects of inquiry. Methodology is in the social world. For example, the more freedom is granted to the evaluator, the more confidentiality has to be assured to informants, and the less the liberty of evaluators to make their own interpretations of the information. Confidentiality demands clearance from informants (Pring, Simons, this volume) which constrains evaluator's decisions on the content, timing and audiences for reports. This tension, between the 'right to privacy' and the 'right to know' (McDonald 1974) is discussed by Pring, Simons and Adelman in this volume.

"Independence" is used in two senses in this book, relfecting the recent history of evaluation outlined above. Lawrence Stenhouse (this volume) contrasts independence with the accountability of the evaluator towards the curriculum developers with whom he/she is implicated. Stenhouse maintains that evaluation is integral to curriculum development, for curriculum development must be complemented and informed by curriculum research. Stenhouse does not hold that evaluation, in the context of curriculum development, should be a field of endeavour in its own right, one in which independence is contrasted with co-option rather than accountability. However, both co-option and accountability shade into complicity and here the inadequacy of the idea and the term "independence" becomes clear. Those evaluators who consider evaluation a field in its own right are inclined to agree with House (1980) that the evaluator has the obligation to persuade, by clarifying alternatives, opening to options, informing and, through persuasion, to ask for informed decisions. In this view the evaluator is not co-opted into any interest group but takes on the responsibility of nurturing the relationship between individual and community towards participatory democracy. This is not independence as aloofness, as disinterest or objectivity (as this is used to signify "uncontaminated") but recognition of an involvement and indeed, an obligation of the evaluator as informed citizen engaged, not in party or power politics, but in the politics of emancipation of consciousness. The means and contents of persuasion used by the evaluator are not derived from ethical imperatives (Pring, this volume), nor from consensual norms but from an effort to consider and understand the consequences of actions. The evaluator in this view is more like a utilitarian after Mill than an idealist after Kant, more like a thoughtful practitioner than one who seeks to confirm theory.

It is difficult to maintain this emphasis on process, on the politics and ethics, the preconditions and procedures, rather than on "new" methodological procedures and techniques which inevitably become ossified as they become institutionalised. Two cases of this come to mind, that of illuminative evaluation (Parlett, M. and Hamilton, D., 1972), now taken as a prerogative to engage in qualitative field work and triangulation (Adelman, 1981) used as an end, rather than a means of pursuing inter-subjectivity in the context of a larger enquiry.

To some extent the evaluation approach that is favoured by the evaluator makes the evaluator more or less vulnerable to the contradictions of other persons politics. Where the approach is "objectivist", the methods of data collection and analysis and the criteria upon which judgements of the worth are made, are explicit from the beginning. House (1980) includes as "objectivist" approaches systems analysis, behavioural objectives, decision making (CIPP) (Stufflebeam, 1971) and goal-free evaluation (Scriven, 1973). Whatever the general suspicions and threat that evaluation poses for the evaluated, these objectivist approaches pre-specify components of the evaluator's role. The evaluated can prepare their strategies for reciprocating the evaluator's enquiries. In "subjectivist" approaches, for instance, those of "case studies" (Simons, H., 1980), "quasi-legal" (Owens, 1973), and "art criticism" (Eisner, E., 1979), the evaluator depends on establishing a role and identity which would foster and sustain collaboration with the evaluated. These "subjectivist" approaches rely on being able to express the different viewpoints and valuings of the evaluated and, to vidicate the collaboration, to report both in form and content in a way that the evaluated understand and realise as pertinent to their practices.

The evaluator's autonomy and impartiality are not within the immediate control of the evaluator, but are dependant on the evaluation approach chosen. Whatever the evaluation approach, the evaluator has to take into account the forms of management and lines of accountability within the instituion, system or project. For the most part those structures already exist before the evaluator beings work and I call these structures the "pre-conditions" (Adelman, 1980). How the evaluator establishes and sustains a role within those pre-conditional structures I think of as part of the evaluation procedures. The evaluator ignores pre-conditions and procedures at his/her peril. For it is not from evaluation methods or, as some would wish to dignify them with the term "theory", that evaluation comes to be done, but by taking into account forms of management and accountability and the inter-personal politics that partly arise from the evaluator's position within these structures. I believe, like Jules

4

Henry (1954), that the formal structure of an organisation defines the limits of reciprocity as much, or more, than ones personal beliefs and feelings.

The evaluator in forming a role within the organisation, gradually accumulates through inter-personal relationships and documentary evidence, the organisation's tendencies and contradictions in terms of aspects of these three change strategies. The evaluator cannot presume too much about the nature of the organisation before beginning the evaluation. Only through inter-personal contacts and by deferring judgement, by sustaining impartiality, can the evaluator maintain adequate awareness of the nature of the organisation. However, at some time or other contradictions become patterned and the differentiation and distribution of knowledge and power becomes clearer. Some people, not necessarily those in formal positions in the structure, have crucial knowledge and power, whilst others are less significant in defining and regulating the accountability and management.

Eraut suggests (this volume) that there is a congruence between evaluation and accountability (a characteristic that social research rarely shares) for evaluation usually follows after legislation and resources for programs have been decided. Evaluators do not engage in the construction of the propositions that underly the programs. They test and comment on these as part of the work of evaluation. By contrast (as Jamieson (this volume) indicates), there are remarkably few sociologists or anthropologists who have directly engaged with such systems of accountability during their research; notable amongst these are Gouldner, Wright-Mills, Burns and H.S. Becker and anthropologists like Mead, Barnes and Bailey.

Essentially it is more difficult for an evaluator to appeal to codes that are broadly supported within an academic discipline. Without an appeal to an academic discipline the evaluator in political circumstances produces reports that are closely linked to the struggle taking place. McLaughlin (1975) summarises these problems succintly:

> "Evaluation embraces two separate dimensions. It is both a logic of enquiry and a part of a complex system of social and political relations".

Drawing on their considerable experience, the authors of this book consider these relationships between the politics, the ethics and the logic of enquiry that comprise evaluation.

NOTES

1. Prof. H. Berlak of Washington University, St. Louis, has provided me with the following note:

> "The School/University programme for research and development was established jointly be the Harvard Graduate School of Education and several co-operating suburban school authorities in Boston in the early 1950's.

By 1959 an inter-related set of projects and programmes in curriculum development, pedagogical research, elementary school structure and change and role re-definition were under way. Associated with these projects were Ralph Moser, Robert Goldhammer, Judson Schaplin, Joe Grannis, Don Oliver and J.P. Shaver. But the time evaluation as a separate field of endeavour began to evolve, these and other projects in the Boston area (such as Project Physics, Zacharias) foreshadowed, in their internal controversies, the ethical problems that began to be made public when evaluation emerged as a field in its own right. The ethical questions include the rights of pupils, community teachers and parents. Some of these debates are reflected in Shaplin, J.B. and Olds H.E. "Team Teaching". Several people involved in this curriculum development and evaulation were taken into the Office of Education during this period with Keppel as Commissioner".

2. Title I of the Elementary Secondary Education Act of 1975 was to quote Silver, H. (1983) "Part of a wide ranging attack on the 'root causes of poverty in the midst of plenty' and represented the widely-held belief that poverty, having been discovered, would now soon be abolished".

REFERENCES

Adelman, Clem (1980) Some Dilemmas of institutional evaluation and their relationship to preconditions and procedures. In: Politics and ethics of case study. No. 7 Case Study Methods, ERM 881. Readings 41-46. Deakin University, Victoria.

Adelman, Clem (1981) On First Hearing. In: Uttering, Muttering: Collecting, Using and Reporting Talk for Social and Educational Research. Grant McIntyre. London. pp 78-97.

Eisner, E. (1979) The Educational Imagination. Macmillan, New York.

Henry, Jules (1954) The formal and social structure of a psychiatric hospital. Psychology XVII pp 139-152.

House, Ernest R. (1980) Evaluating with Validity. Sage Publications, Beverley Hills, California.

McDonald, B. (1974) Evaluation and the Control of Education, reprinted in (SAFARI 1) Innovation, Evaluation Research and the problem of control: Some interim papers, Centre for Applied Research in Education, University of East Anglia, Norwich. In: Tawney, David (Ed.) (1976) Curriculum Evaluation Today: Trends and Implications. Schools Council, Macmillan, London.

McLaughlin, M.W. (1975) Education and Reform. Ballinger Pub. Co. Cambridge, Mass.

Owens, T.R. (1973) Educational evaluation by adversary proceeding. In House, E.R. (Ed.) School Evaluation. McCutchan, Berkeley.

Parlett, Malcolm and Hamilton, David (1972) Evaluation as Illumination: A New Approach to the Study of Innovatory

Programs. Centre for Research in the Educational Sciences. University of Edinburgh. Occasional Paper 9.

Rippey, Robert M. (1973) Studies in Transactional Evaluation. McCutchan Publishing Corp. Berkeley, California. Scriven Michael (1967) "The Methodology of Evaluation" (1967) in R.E. Stake Perspectives on Curriculum Evaluation, Educational Research Association, Monograph Series on Curriculum Evaluation. No. 1, Rand McNally, Chicago.

Scriven, Michael (1973) Goal-free evaluation. In House, Ernest R. School evaluation: the Politics and Process. McCutchan Pub. Corp., Berkeley, California, pp 319-328.

Shaplin, Judson Tiffany and Olds, Henry E. (Eds.) (1964) Team Teaching. Harper and Row, London.

Silver, Harold (1983) Education against poverty: interpreting British and American politics in the 1960's and 1970's. In Silver, Harold Education as History. Methuen and Co. London, pp. 257-278.

Stake, R.E. (1967) Perspectives on Curriculum Evaluation: Educational Research Association, Monograph Series on Curriculum Evaluation. No. 1, Rand McNally, Chicago.

Stake, R.E. (1974) Responsive Evaluation (revised) in New Trends in Education, Institute of Education, University of Goteborg. No. 35.

Stufflebeam, Daniel L. (Ed.) (1971) Educational Evaluation and Decision Making. F.E. Peacock for Phi Delta Kappa National Study Committee on Evaluation: Itasca, Ill.

Walker, Rob. (Nov. 1974) Classroom Research: A View from Safari. In: Safari. Innovation, Evaluation, Research and the Problem of Control. Centre for Applied Research in Education, University of East Anglia, Norwich.

Chapter 1

CONFIDENTIALITY AND THE RIGHT TO KNOW

Richard Pring

Introduction

Evaluation of what happens in schools requires access to information and the right to report on what is observed so that different people – employers, parents, curriculum developers – can be better informed. But this may not in all cases be in the best interests of the teachers and the children. Moral problems arise concerning the right of researchers and evaluators to know what they need to know for their particular purposes. Some of these moral problems can be anticipated, and safeguards established, through a code of conduct, but such a code must remain fairly general and can be no substitute for moral responsibility on the part of the evaluator and for appropriate relationships of trust between evaluator and teacher.

The Source of the Problem

There is a lot of criticism, quite understandably, of the secrecy with which the affairs of public institutions such as schools, local education authorities, or Government departments and committees are conducted. There is a need for more openness to ensure that decisions are made in an informed manner and that these institutions are properly accountable to the people they serve. To many therefore there is a prima facie case for claiming the 'right to know' and for the exercise of this right through a more thorough evaluation of schools and other institutions. Often this right is insisted upon even when the subsequent enquiry and revelation are said to damage the people or institutions into which the enquiry is made. The problem is a complex and difficult ethical one – the right of some to know versus the right of others to preserve a degree of privacy even in matters that affect the public good. The complexity of this issue is apparent in many of the papers in this book. In what follows I shall do no more than examine what 'the right to know' means and indicate why, in any programme of evaluation, it should be made conditional upon the realisation of other values.

8

The Right to Know

Broadly speaking, ethical theories (and therefore the way issues are tackled from an ethical point of view) tend to fall into one of two camps. First there are those that stress the intrinsic value of particular activities, irrespective of the consequences. Secondly, there are those that judge the value of what is done much more by reference to the consequences. Of course, most ethical positions have (and must have) a bit of both, but there are differences of emphasis, and these differences seem particularly relevant to consideration of the ethical problems in evaluation, and in particular to the respect to be attached to confidentiality.

The insistence upon 'rights' falls very much in the first kind of ethical position. When the Americans asserted that all men had an equal right to life, liberty and the pursuit of happiness, they appealed, not to the beneficial consequences of having such a right acknowledged, but to self-evident principles. And indeed the view that certain rights are 'natural', and as such can be appealed to in any criticism of society's actual laws, practices, and institutions, has been a popular aspect of political argument. In the context of education, we hear frequent talk of the rights of various groups - parents, children, teachers, employers. Furthermore, since the extent of this talk is often inversely proportional to the extent of agreement about these rights, we can presume that often it is an appeal to rights which, because not recognised, are somehow there 'in a state of nature', existing whether agreed upon or not.

The current concern for accountability has, as one might expect, resulted in many 'natural right' types of claim. When we ask why schools should be more accountable to parents, taxpayers, professional colleagues, children, employers, the answer often is that these bodies have certain rights - natural rights in that they are not written into any laws or rules and have not been agreed upon and in that they 'arise from' the particular social relationships that exist between the agents of schooling on the one hand and these different groups on the other. Thus parents, by virtue of special responsibilities for their children, claim special rights which are often not fully recognised by schools. Roughly these rights might be of two kinds: firstly the right to have more information about what happens in schools; secondly, the right to intervene in the light of that information. I, as a parent, feel that I ought to be fully informed about what happens to my children in school. I also feel that if I do not like what I am told, I ought to have certain powers to help me change what I do not like. It is a short step to transform such feelings into talk about rights.

On the other hand such rights, claimed on behalf of parents, employers, administrators, professional bodies must be set against the other rights claimed by teachers as professionals. First, they would claim, as in the case of priests or doctors, the right not to release information that has been gained in pursuit of their professional tasks. Secondly, they would claim the right to pursue their own judgment and therefore draw upon the special insights afforded by experience and training. Perhaps such rights, arising from the professionalism of teachers, would not be held to be 'natural ones', but they often seem preciously like them since professionalism in the context of teaching is ill-defined, without any agreed code of conduct or set of obligations.

A major problem that I see therefore in the current interest in making schools and teachers more accountable lies precisely in the rather foggy area of establishing rights and obligations, where there is no agreement on what these are and where there is no well-established social tradition that can be appealed to. In the absence of either, we are left with some sort of appeal to natural rights with all the problems that that entails, for 'rights' (especially 'natural rights') are most certainly what in current philososphical language might be called 'an essentially contestable concept'.

I talk of it as 'an essentially contestable concept' because (1) the meaning of 'rights' is disagreed upon and indeed contested, (2) these disagreements incorporate fairly fundamental differences of view about what is of value, (3) there seems ultimately no way of settling these differences. Hence, arguments about 'rights' so often contain appeals to different political or moral values. And this was never so true as in the present assertion of rights by parents or by the taxpayer or by any group of people – the rights both to know more about schools and to intervene where what is known is not liked.

In one sense, 'right' is not 'essentially contestable'. There are certain logical features of its use that any competent speaker of the English language implicitly subscribes. And indeed a great deal of philosophical literature has marked out these characteristics – the nature of the relationship between rights and duties, the classification of different kinds of rights, the function of claims to certain rights, the connection between rights, responsibilities, freedoms, and so on. To say, for example, that somebody has the right to something implies that there is some rule that establishes mutual obligations. If A has a right to X then somebody else has an obligation to make sure that A is not prevented from having X. Rules may be explicit in a legal system or they may be implicit in a social custom or a widely shared traditional way of behaving. But where there are no such laws and no such agreed understandings, it is difficult to make sense of there being rules establishing mutual obligation; and thus the claim to there being 'rights' prior to such agreement seems a spurious one. Rights are not the sort of thing that can be observed. They do not hang around the world, as it were, waiting to be discovered. Hence, many of the current claims to have a right to know or to intervene do not seem irreconcilable by purely rational means, the different definitions of right that reflect them seem essentially contestable. 'The right to know' is often a false claim, since there are rarely such established rights, either in legislation or in social practice. It is therefore much more a slogan, a part of the rhetoric which might however result one day in the establishment of such rights. 'Right' is essentially contestable not in its broad formal features but in the substantive claims made under its banner.

These considerations are particularly relevant to some of the claims made on behalf of curriculum evaluation. MacDonald distinguishes between bureaucratic, autocratic, and democratic evaluation, and there has, since then, been no doubting the anxiety with which some evaluators wish to be seen in the democratic camp. Few of us indeed would wish to be called bureaucrats or autocrats, since these words have a pejorative ring to them. But upon analysis what characterises the democratic evaluator seems to be the recognition of the basic right to know. As MacDonald explains, "the key concepts of democratic evaluation are 'confidentiality', 'negotiation', and 'accessibility'", but "the key justificatory concept is ' the right to know'". It should be noted that the key justificatory concept is not that of making the system a happier one, or of promoting better education, or of enabling to learn more efficiently, or of respecting the aspirations of parents. It may be of course that 'democratic evaluation' or 'providing an information service to the whole community' might promote these worthy aims. On the other hand it may not. But whether it does or it doesn't would not matter to the democratic evaluator, as described, since the right to know is basic –indeed it is the key justificatory concept.

My hesitation in readily joining the democratic camp, is that I cannot, for reasons given above, see how the 'right to know' is 'basic' or is a 'key justificatory concept'. To repeat what I said, in the absence of agreed social norms or rules that encapsulate such rights, then it is difficult to see what form of existence they have. And clearly there are no such agreements – except, by definition, amongst 'democratic evaluators'. That is not to say that a democratic mode of evaluation cannot be justified. Quite clearly it may be defined for a variety of reasons as the most appropriate means of achieving certain valued ends. But that is not the same as asserting the basic right to know. To justify the right to know as a means to an end raises the ethical questions about evaluation in a quite different way. It allows room for the bureaucrat, and even for the autocrat, since, having got rid of basic rights, it can approach each situation more pragmatically, less dogmatically.

One kind of argument is however worth attending to. John Stuart Mill in his essay "On Liberty" argues thus for preserving and extending freedom of discussion:

" . . . the peculiar evil of silencing the expression of an opinion is, that it is robbing the human race; posterity as well as the existing generation; those who dissent from the opinion, still more than those who hold it. If the opinion is right, they are deprived of the opportunity of exchanging error for truth; if wrong, they lose, what is almost as great a benefit, the clearer perception and livelier impression of truth, produced by its collision with error". (p. 142)

Of course, the accessibility of information is a precondition of discussing properly any opinion. There is on Mill's argument a prima facie case therefore for establishing the right to know as somehow a basic one, if either the eradication of error or the sharpening up of what is true is held to be of value - as indeed it must be by anyone who seriously engages in some particular enquiry. The intellectual life has its own peculiar virtues - not cooking the books is one, being properly informed is another. There are no absolute certainties, and thus, faced with the continual possibility of self-deception or of wrong conclusions, one should welcome rather than spurn the well-informed critic. The peculiarity of Mill's argument lies in its pointing to necessary conditions of the proper pursuit of enquiry, and the necessary value attached to enquiry by anyone who is seriously asking these question. The 'right to know' may not exist, like mountains and rivers, independently of the social rules that man has created and that established mutual relationships of obligations and rights. On the other hand, such social rules must necessarily be agreed upon where getting at the truth is a valued activity.

Why then do I still hesitate to concede this basic right? There are several reasons. Firstly, the right to know seems most defensible where the connection between such a right and the sincere pursuit of disinterested enquiry is clear. But not always is there such a clear connection. People engage in enquiries for a variety of reasons - some to confirm their prejudices (and is it not the case that false theories can be confirmed, given enough information to choose from?), others to pursue their small vendettas, yet others for undesirable political ends. The information industry is as much the servant of interested parties as it is the servant of those who in a disinterested way are keen to know more.

Would I be prepared to concede the 'right to know' to someone whose motives I had good grounds to suspect or whose record in misinterpreting what is known is notorious? Where such doubts about the right to know remain, I cannot see it as a basic right - the key justificatory principle, requiring no appeal to further more fundamental principles. It may be conceded in particular cases precisely because of the arguments that Mill puts so cogently. But such concession, if made wisely, would be weighed against other considerations.

A lot in practice rests on these considerations. Under the misguided belief in the right to know - the right not only of oneself but also of the wider public -schools have been observed, teachers and pupils interviewed, classroom conversations and activities minutely examined, and all reported upon to the public at large, of the consequences to that school or to those teachers and pupils. It is an ethic of absolute rights, rather than an ethic of consequences. The answer to this, of course, is not to deny the right to know, but to see that right as something that needs to be established in particular cases. Its establishment, of course, will require the acceptance of a set of rules that incorporate that right, as well as obligations upon which it is made conditional.

Conditions for granting 'the right to know'

The acceptance of certain obligations upon which the concession of the right to know is made conditional, provides the main reason why I cannot see that right as basic - as so self-evident that the person, group, or institution should immediately expose himself or itself to the public gaze. And what these obligations are - how they are formulated - would depend upon the circumstances. None the less, certain general principles might be suggested for general airing. Let us test these through a particular example.

In Britain the Social Science Research Council agreed to fund a three year study by the University of London Institute of Education (Gipps, C., Goldstein, H. 1983) into the effect of the monitoring of achievement in schools on the educational system. The object of the study was to assess the influence of testing programmes on schools and on educational policies at local and national levels, but it would have a particular interest in the effects of the work of the Assessment of Performance Unit. The Assessment of Performance Unit, like the National Assessment of Educational Performance in the U.S.A., is concerned with monitoring pupil performance across the country in different curriculum areas on a light sampling basis, but unlike National Assessment of Educational Performance it is firmly rooted in a Government department and therefore more vulnerable to the influences of central government. In pursuing this interest the study was to evaluate the 'political' context of the APU programme - 'how researchers, professional groups, local education authorities and other special interest groups have reacted to the APU, and how the APU committees and research teams function'. It would also focus upon the effect of APU and local education authority testing programmes on the school system.

In pursuing this research, the team wished to monitor discussions of some of the working and steering groups. How should those groups have responded to this request? Firstly, there is no doubting the importance of some research of this kind - not because of any basic right to know (I repeat, the very conception of 'basic rights' is meaningless in the absence of particular agreements, and it is the getting of agreements that is precisely at issue), but because of the possible consequences to social welfare of the work of such bodies as the APU. Hence, in general terms the importance of discussion of these issues should be recognised and the essential condition of such discussion -viz the availability of relevant data - acknowledged, and indeed that exactly is what the Department of Education and Science agreed to.

But there is a world of difference between such general approval and its detailed application. Ethical arguments, despite impressions given in undergraduate courses, rarely arise at the general level, but only in their detailed working out. That cruelty is wrong might generally be agreed upon; that this or that particular action is cruel, or that, if cruel, it is permissible in extenuating circumstances is where the disagreement arises. It is in relating the general principle to the concrete case, and in deciding upon the exceptions, that moral disagreement really bites, and it is the sort of disagreement therefore that ethical considerations need to get to grips with. Hence, the ethical questions in this instance concern not the right to know as such, but how much should be accessible and under what conditions.
And, in sorting this out, one is not acknowledging natural rights; rather is one negotiating what the reciprocal rights and obligations should be.

Let me suggest therefore certain general considerations that might provide some formal framework of principle within which details might be decided – and let us think of it, too, in the context of a particular group whose work is being monitored. What obligations should they wish to see placed upon the 'researcher' or 'evaluator' upon which the right to know would be conditional?

(a) The researcher would set out clearly the <u>kinds</u> of knowledge that he wanted. It is of course impossible in research to anticipate all kinds of information that you want, but the continuing opportunity to renegotiate the terms of contract (of agreed rights and obligations) could be secured.

(b) The researcher has an obligation to show, throughout the research, his 'papers' – i.e. the data collected (<u>or selected</u>) and the interpretation of that data.

(c) The researcher, both at the beginning and throughout, would be open to cross-examination by the group about the research – its main objectives, its research methodology, its political implications, the data it collects and the interpretation upon that data. Such an obligation arises particularly from the ill-conceived nature of some research, and from the often-prevailing but naive philosophical view that 'knowledge' is a sort of datum not in essence affected by the style of research, its main purposes, or its underlying political motivation.

(d) The research is obliged to incorporate in his findings the reply, if any, of those researched.

The above considerations were a development of my first reason for hesitating to concede the right to know as basic. In a few words, that reason is that the connection betwen making available all that is relevant on the one hand and disinterested enquiry on the other is not in all cases simple and straightforward. And accesibility to available knowledge therefore is by no means a natural right but has to be established as a worthy aim, after the wider implications of knowing have been scrutinised. All this, of course, should be set against the argument of Mill which makes a <u>prima facie</u> case of openness rather than concealment.

There is however a second reason closely connected, and to some extent touched upon, in principle (c) above. The slogan 'the right to know' suffers not only from the essentially contestable nature of 'right' but also from the ambiguities surrounding the word 'know'. Knowledge does of course refer to those sets of beliefs that are not only true but that one has good grounds for believing. The right to know must include the opportunities to put on a firmer footing one's beliefs and to rid oneself of whatever is false. The right to know would require the best possible conditions for thorough critical scrutiny of what is believed. Only that, as one might argue, which has survived such criticism is worthy of knowing –for anything else may not be knowedge at all, only the delusions of a fanciful imagination. On the other hand, what we know is expressible in propositions, and ultimately in bodies of knowledge or interrelated sets of propositions that are the product of particular enquiries. To have knowledge requires understanding and understanding often requires in turn a grasp of the interconnections that relate one part of the picture to another. It also often requires some participation in those very enquiries in terms of which that 'knowledge' is to be understood. Forgetting this, one is in constant danger of confusing the possession of blobs of so called knowledge with knowing itself. This is, of course, a difficult matter to be clear about. But at least it means this – that the exposure to particular facts or to particular statements or to a selection from the data can so easily distort an understanding of what then is made public, for it removes that which is to be known from the context in which it must be understood or from the process to which it is logically related as product. It is for this reason that I would want to link the right to know with a reciprocal obligation to permit enlargments and explanations from those who are researched. The sum of what we know is more than the sum of atomic propositions, corresponding to a range of atomic facts. It involves interpretation, theoretical assumptions, reference to the peculiarities of context. And these therefore must be as explicit as possible in what is publicly revealed.

The final reason for hesitating to concede, without further justification, the right to know is that so often the exercise of such a right would clash with other values which prima facie seem as, or indeed more, fundamental. It is a mistake, in the attempt to be more systematic in ethical thinking, to look for some hierarchy of principle, duties, or values, such that just one supreme principle remains as the ultimate court of appeal – whether it be the maximisation of happiness or obedience to some authority or some form of enlightenment. On the contrary, there is a range of different values and principles and prima facie duties. And it is the character of the moral life that where there is a clash of such values and principles there is no 'higher level' set of principles to appeal to in order to resolve that clash. Examples of such a clash would be where keeping a promise can only result in hurting a person. There is no rule of thumb for resolving the difficulty, just as there is no way of quantifying the seriousness of the promise and the degree of hurt.

Respect for another person is of course a very general principle, so general in fact that it is safely without much content. On the other hand, it indicates a general orientation towards the other person, a recognition that he is a centre of conscious life and feeling, an acceptance of his responsibility for what he does, and a determination to protect and to support that life. It is reflected in a range of lower-level principles such as not betraying trust, trying not to hurt, keeping promises, and (more positively) helping him to accept responsibility for his actions. It is not difficult to see how 'the right to know' can so easily clash with this general principle of respect. Firstly, it can require an intrusion into the private life of the individual. Secondly, it could mean betraying trust and confidence. At this point we have to consider, albeit briefly, the interests of the individual weighed against those of the public.

Private and Public Interest

The distinction between the private life and the public life of an individual is a difficult and blurred one, just as Mill's distinction between public and private morality, essential to his principle of liberty, becomes exceedingly fuzzy when analysed in detail. On the other hand, however blurred the boundaries there do seem to be clear cases of activities on each side of the boundary. Nose picking after 10 p.m., no matter how repulsive some may find it, would be part of Blogg's private life, and he would quite understandably resent the publication of this in the daily papers. Whereas, if he were a teacher, his advocacy of corporal punishment or his inability to spell correctly would be, quite rightly, of public interest. The right to know would need to attend to this distinction which quite clearly it does not in a lot of journalism. I say 'attend to' on purpose, because where exactly the distinction is drawn between the public and the private is not possible to say in advance of particular cases. But that there is a distinction to be made does put restrictions upon 'the right to know'.

Furthermore this distinction does become more difficult to define given the political context of decisions which affect many people. That I willingly concede. There is a close connection between making people and institutions more accountable and political questions about the distribution of power and control. And it would be wrong to treat the ethical issue between the right to know and confidentiality in a totally apolitical manner. That is why in matters of considerable political concern, such as the work of the APU, the case for complete openness of committee deliberations should be made at the earliest stages of discussion and the area of confidentiality limited quite explicity. The balance in other words between competing ethical principles, and between the private and the public, must relate to the political significance of the authorities or institutions being evaluated.

Trust and Confidentiality

The betrayal of trust raises more significant issues which are just as complicated. Clear cases of betrayal of trust are where a promise is broken. There is of course something very peculiar about the obligation to keep promises. Where that obligation is not recognised the very meaning of 'making a promise' disintegrates. And furthermore little value can be put upon promises where it is understood that promises can be broken should the person promising, upon reflection, believe that this would be for the general good. Keeping promises would seem to be a prima facie duty. However, the trust that is built up between evaluator and the people evaluated, on the basis of which information is given and intelligence gained, is rarely made explicit in actual promises. It is much more a matter of implicit trusting with information, putting oneself in a vulnerable position. This respect for the other person as vulnerable and as having entered into a relationship of trust puts considerable constraints upon the evaluator however much public importance he attaches to the information he has.

It is out of respect for this particular value, as against the 'right to know', that as far as I can see so much attention has been given in recent literature to 'negotiation'. The particular difficulties of spelling this notion out in practice have been well analysed by Helen Simons (1977) in "Building a Social Contract: negotiation, participation, and portrayal in condensed field research", in particular the difficulties in protecting the person being evaluated even after faithful adherence to agreed procedures of negotiation. Somehow a contract is not enough. Such a contract has to be suffused with a spirit of respect for the other than can never be captured in a contract alone.

I am not in a position to develop this aspect of the problem. There is something odd about the idea of negotiation. It is a metaphor taken from business, and like all metaphors it plays its part but has its limitations. Particularly, however, it seems odd in an area where matters of truth and falsity are concerned, and there does at times seem to be some confusion between negotiating the release of 'knowledge' and negotiating what that knowledge consists in. To follow that particular point is beyond the scope of this paper, but it touches upon the main topic because the right to know, if established, would be limited by, amongst other things, the principle of not betraying trust and confidence. Certainly this would be most directly applicable to the release of information. But it could also be extended to interpretation put upon that information. What must one agree to, or 'negotiate', prior to making public one's evaluation, in order to keep within the bounds of confidence - the information given, the sense given to the information, the conclusions drawn? What certainly is clear from Helen Simons' account is that the further one extends the notion of confidentiality and the consequent obligation to negotiate, the greater must be the constraints in establishing any right to know. I would have thought that confidentiality had a strong claim where one is concerned with the release of basic data, obtained for example in interview or as a result of trust. But it has a much less formidable claim as soon as one moves away from that to interpretation and to drawing conclusions.

Nonetheless, the word 'negotiation', inadequate metaphor though it may be, does remind us once again that drawing the boundary between the right to know and preserving confidentiality cannot be seen outside a political context - outside, that is, of a context in which power and influence are exercised over people. In the last section I referred to the prima facie case for limiting the area of confidentiality in areas of considerable political significance such as in the work of the APU. Knowledge is an important ingredient in the balance of power, and 'negotiating' contracts with an evaluator can be seen as a sort of 'trading' in political power which in many cases will be a consequence of a shift in the distribution of knowledge.

This does nonetheless pose very real problems for the evaluator when he takes seriously the ethical context in which he pursues his enquiry. I have throughout this paper failed to distinguish clearly between research and evaluation, and yet this may be an important distinction for our purposes. Evaluation studies, unlike central cases of research, are concerned not so much with theory building or generalisation as with a grasp of the particular and with improved practice and it could be seriously affected if particular episodes, interactions, relationships, and differing perceptions which constitute 'the particular' get omitted from the record. There is a prima facie case for more access to detail in evaluation studies than there is in much research. In other words, there are limits to how much negotiation is acceptable if the aims of the evaluator are to be achieved and this would need to be taken into account in drawing up any code of practice or principles of procedure.

Conclusions

In this paper I have examined briefly the force of the notion 'the right to know'. I share the view that, all things being equal, openness, availability of relevant information, and public criticism are, as Mill argues, good for getting rid of error as well as for sharpening one's perception of the truth. To that extent there is a prima facie case for establishing a right to know. But such rights do need to be established - they are in no way basic. And to establish them requires some examination of the consequences of establishing such a right in particular cases. Maybe the right to know all (or this or that) will lead to undesirable results. Maybe it will clash with other principles such as confidentiality. The main thing however is that, as in most moral matters, whether the right should be given and over what area it should be extended need to be argued in the context of particular cases.

REFERENCES

Gipps, Caroline and Goldsteing, Harvey. (1983) Monitoring Children Heinemann Ed. London.

MacDonald B. (1976) "Evaluation and the Control of Education" in Tawney D. (Ed) Curriculum Evaluation Today: Trends and Implications, London: Macmillan.

Mill J. S. (1859) On Liberty, published in Warnock M. (Ed) (1962) Utilitarianism, London: Collins.

Simons, H. (1977) "Building a Social Contract: Negotiation and Participation in Concerned Fieldwork Research" In: Norris, N. (Ed.) Safari: theory and practice. C.A.R.A Occasional Paper no. 4. University of East Anglia, Norwich.

Chapter 2

METHODOLOGY AND ETHICS

John Elliott

    At the annual conference of the British Educational Research Association in 1975 there was a symposium on 'teacher participation in research'. One of the contributors was Barry MacDonald. He argued that practitioners ought to have control over an 'outside researcher's' access to information about their practices, and the conditions governing its public release. This view created a considerable uproar in the audience. MacDonald's response was that practitioners 'owned the facts about their lives'. Many of those present found such a response totally unsatisfactory arguing that it compromised the researcher's responsibility to publish the truth about the situation under investigation.

    I find the views expressed by MacDonald's opponents understandable in terms of the positivist paradigm educational researchers have borrowed from the natural sciences. The basic premise underlying this paradigm is that 'true facts' about social action exist quite independently of the ways human agents understand the social contexts in which they act. From within this interpretative framework human beings are conceived as passive objects whose behaviour is as causally explicable by antecedent events as phenomena in the natural world. Viewed as such they cannot become 'objects' of ethical concern. Science and ethics are held as logically distinct universes of discourse.

    Positivistic knowledge of social phenomena, as Habermas (1971) points out, is constituted by the practical interests of instrumental action. By positing human behaviour as causally determined, positivistic knowledge becomes readily translatable into technical rules for manipulating that behaviour in order to achieve desired ends. It comes to possess instrumental value as a means of exercising power over human beings. No wonder then that it is a view of social knowledge favoured by governments who wish to exercise power over the citizenry; whether it be to do them 'good' or 'harm'.

    According to Barnes (1977) it is only recently, since World War II, that governments "have begun to envisage seriously the possibility of social engineering, the conscious and deliberate alteration of the parameters of social life so as to bring about some socially desired and scientifically predicted end." Positivistic knowledge has become a source of political power as governments have become more important and sought to control areas of social life previously considered 'private'. This conception of social science knowledge as power has also resulted in increasing government control over researchers' access to funds, the kinds of problems they address themselves to, and the methodologies they employ. 'Academic freedom' or 'independent research' is a difficult value for poor hardworking social researchers to subscribe to. As Barnes points out "The social scientist is no longer the elite gentleman of private means but is a propertyless professional dependent on support from a sponsor". The decline of available funds from independent agencies, and the growth of government sponsored research, ensures a 'brighter' future for positivist methodology than some of us hoped for. It is a future in which there is little room for ethical concern.

Hollis (1977) contrasts a social science operating with a model of man as Plastic man with one which views him as Autonomous man. Plastic Man is passive, "a programmed feed back system, whose inputs, outputs and inner workings can be given many interpretations", while Autonomous Man is active, having "some species of substantial self within". It is when the social researcher views social action as the product of that substantial self that the practitioner becomes an object of ethical concern, and methodology becomes inseparable from ethics.

Autonomous Man creates his own acts out of his own constructions of social reality; an interpretative framework of values and beliefs which define his obligations to others, and theirs to him. The way he describes these acts is conditioned by his interpretation of the social context in which they occur. For example, the description 'I am asserting that' etc. consists of more than simply 'uttering a statement'. It implies that I have placed myself under an obligation to speak the truth then I wouldn't describe my utterance as an 'assertion'. Autonomous man describes his actions in terms of the extent to which they realise or fail to realise the values to which he commits himself.

It is only from the perspective of Autonomous Man that a knowledge of social action becomes viewed as the private property of practitioners. MacDonald's case rests on the view that facts about social action are a matter of 'private' rather than 'public' knowledge. Truth-criteria are relative to the different interpretative frameworks social agents employ to guide their conduct. Hence, for MacDonald's 'democratic evaluator', (MacDonald and Walker 1977), 'truth is multiple'. Such a view of truth is grounded in a researcher's experience of what Cupitt (1976) calls 'the interpretative plasticity of the world', the fact that "the world of our experience is seemingly willing to lend itself to interpretation in terms of a great variety of different programmes" (frameworks). It is an experience which depends upon the existence of a pluralistic-democracy in which people not only differ with respect to the ways they interpret the social world but are given the freedom to act in the light of these interpretations without interference from central government. As government becomes more important and the sphere of 'the private' becomes increasingly eroded, we can expect this experience of 'interpretative plasticity' to become rarer amongst social researchers, particularly in the light of their dependence on government sponsorship for funds.

Since what counts as the true facts about social action is relative to the interpretative frameworks which agents employ, there is a sense in which they are in the best position to say what they are. Thus giving practitioners the right to control public access to 'the true facts' about their conduct is not simply an ethical option to be considered in addition to methodology. It is also a methodological requirement; a logically necessary condition of public access to 'the facts'.

From this view of social knowledge and truth MacDonald derives his methodology of democratic evaluation. The role of 'the outside evaluator' is that of a 'neutral broker' who negotiates accounts of their activities with a variety of 'interest groups', and fosters an exchange of information between them. In this way different 'interest groups' can come to understand each other's activities, and appreciate the different interpretative frameworks which render them intelligible. Such an approach appears to be constituted by a practical interest in fostering mutual understanding and tolerance. However, these methodological implications of the premise that practitioners own the facts about their lives are not unproblematic. As Barnes has pointed out, there is a current tendency for certain social groups to draw alternative methodological conclusions from this premise. They would deny any outside researcher's access to their lives on the grounds that he could never understand 'the true facts' and would inevitably misrepresent them.

> 'A man can never understand the woman's point of view, a white can never comprehend what it is like to be black, an atheist cannot realise what it means to have faith in a god.' (Barnes 1977)

This 'no understanding without commitment' position implies that social research can only be conducted for 'insiders' by 'insiders'. If it is valid then we must conclude with Barnes that:

> "the notion of a unified and universal social science begins to disappear, to be replaced by black sociology, white sociology, the sociology of women, the sociology of men, and so on, each with its own impenetrable mystique."

We must also deny the framework of liberal-democratic values by which the democratic evaluator/researcher's methodology is constituted. A researcher can no longer experience 'the interpretative plasticity' of the social world from a social vantage point existing outside the values and beliefs of a particular 'interest' group. His methodology is entirely constituted by the practical interests of the group in which he participates. The 'virtues' of pluralistic understanding, tolerance, and dialogue, vanish.

In my opinion this denial of the possibility of understanding from 'the outside' is related to the growth of the power of governments over their citizenry, and their control over social research. Such a development itself constitutes an erosion of pluralistic liberal democracies. One way of resisting the power of government, exercised through methods of bureaucratic control, and thereby exerting their rights of autonomy, is for groups to resist any public access to their activities, whether it is via research or any other means. The 'no understanding without commitment' argument is perhaps best interpreted as an ideological rationalisation for adopting an insular position in a society where the traditional liberal values of mutual understanding, tolerance, and freedom are being undermined by power struggles and conflict. As an ideology it derives its plausability from the fact that a great deal of sponsored research does misrepresent the activities of practitioners. It does so because positivism has been the dominant paradigm within which it was conducted.

The ethical principle of giving practitioners control over what is to count as 'the true facts' about their activities is therefore not only grounded in the view that they are in the best position to understand them, but also in the view that they can communicate something of their self-understanding to 'outsiders', in a way which does not constitute misunderstanding. Both Barnes (1977) and Hulmes (1979) do not question the view that the self-understanding of 'the insider' is necessarily fuller than that achieved by 'outsiders', whose understanding is always a partial one. In doing so they acknowledge an element of truth in the 'no understanding without commitment' thesis. What they disagree with is the implication that 'understanding' is an all or nothing affair. The difference between 'the insider's' and 'outsider's' understanding appears to be merely one of degree.

However, I would argue that the element of truth in the thesis cited is unfairly played down if one sees the differences in understanding between 'insiders' and 'outsiders' as a matter of degree. There is an important qualititative difference between them; they are distinct kinds of understanding. When 'insiders' assert that there can be 'no understanding without commitment' they are not suggesting 'outsiders' cannot comprehend 'the bald facts' about their activities. Rather they are asserting the logical impossibility of them grasping the meaning of these facts in the way they do themselves. Thus as Brodbeck (1969) argues there is a sense in which I cannot understand what it means to have been a member of the Italian Resistance, because "I have not had the special feelings, emotions, or attitudes that are aroused only by having participated in certain kinds of events." There is a kind of understanding which can only be had by committing oneself to the relevant interpretative framework and entering into the social relationships it prescribes. However, Brodbeck also argues that there is a different sense in which I can understand what it means to be a member of the Italian Resistance; again one which goes beyond a mere grasp of 'the bald facts'. She writes, "The unique phenomenological experience that is the resultant of fear, patriotism, courage, hatred of tyranny, all acting jointly, I do not understand. However, because I understand the meaning of fear, patriotism, and so on, I can understand (in a different sense) what it meant to be a member of the resistance."

The existence of certain constants in human experience – universal feelings, emotions, and attitudes – enables me to empathise with someone whose experience differs from mine; albeit less completely than another who shares it.

This qualitative distinction between two kinds of understanding enables us to reconcile the idea of 'private knowledge' with 'public access'. It also illuminates the research ethic of giving control over public access to that knowledge to 'the insider', as against 'the outside' researcher. The test that 'the outsiders' understanding fairly represents the activities of 'insiders', however partial it is, resides in the latter perceiving it as 'a fair representation'. As Hulmes argues, in the slightly different context of students learning about an 'alien' religious tradition:

> "It is insufficient for the student to convince himself that his study of Islam has brought a measure of understanding, if the expression of that understanding blocks the dialogue between himself and a Muslim. The test of understanding is not so subjective. The test lies in the response the 'understanding' works in the one who stands committed to the tradition being 'understood'."

Hulmes' argument clearly illustrates the link between the ethic of 'giving control' and methodology. The ethic is a necessary condition of testing the objectivity of 'the outsiders' understanding. Hulmes also brings out another methodological aspect of social understanding from 'the outside'. It is developed in personal dialogue with 'insiders'. Hence, the importance MacDonald and Walker (1977) attribute to 'negotiation', in addition to that of 'control', as a key concept in democratic evaluation.

The concept of 'negotiation' highlights the social researcher's responsibility to render the activities of 'insiders' publicly intelligible without misrepresenting their private meanings. Although 'outsiders' can never completely penetrate the private knowledge of 'insiders', they must avoid an over-literal interpretation of 'the facts'. If a researcher confines his task to describing 'the bald facts' he will wrench them out of context, and thereby misrepresent them. In this respect positivist research with its belief in 'naked truth', inevitably misrepresents.

In attempting to 'speak the truth' about the activities of 'insiders', researchers must learn to operate with what Bonhoeffer (1949) called the idea of living truth. He argued that:

> " 'Telling the truth' means something different according to the particular situation in which one stands. Account must be taken of one's relationships at each particular time .. "

He defines truthful speech as expressing the real in words. Reality is not simply expressed in the propositional content of a statement, citing what I have called 'the bald facts', but in its form. Here I think Bonhoeffer is referring to the difference between 'the meaning of what I say' and 'what I mean in what I say'. Truthful speech must accommodate both aspects. Thus in writing about the use of a word, he comments:

"Quite apart from the veracity of its contents, the relation between myself and another man which is expressed in it is in itself either true or untrue. I speak flatteringly or presumptuously or hypocritically without uttering a material untruth; yet my words are nevertheless untrue, because I am disrupting and destroying the reality of the relationship between man and wife, superior and subordinate, etc. . . . It is only the cynic who claims 'to speak the truth' at all times and in all places to all men in the same way, but who, in fact, displays nothing but a lifeless image of the truth."

It is in negotiation with 'insiders' that social researcher's learn 'to speak the truth', by feeding back to them their public translations of private knowledge. Methodology expresses an ethical relationship between 'outsider' and 'insider', and not the application of a battery of 'objective' techniques.

Now it is easy to interpret 'control' and 'negotiation' in terms of researchers allowing practitioners to decide how much of the truth should be told. Bonhoeffer himself acknowledged that his concept of 'living truth' was dangerous because it could easily be misunderstood in such terms. However, he argued that such a danger "must never impel one to abandon this concept in favour of the formal and cynical concept of truth".

MacDonald's democratic evaluation also incorporates giving practitioners blanket 'confidentiality' during the period of data collection, and then 'negotiating' what can be released afterwards. Now this procedure is not necessarily the same as the one I have discussed, yet both are forms of 'giving control' and 'negotiation', and even MacDonald I think confuses them. 'Confidentiality' need imply nothing about how 'the facts' are to be rationally determined. It simply indicates that they will not be publicly released – regardless of questions about their truth. 'Control' in this context need have nothing to do with testing for truth; its point being to protect practitioners against the harmful consequences of release. Similarly, 'negotiation' is ambiguous. It need have little to do with the transformation of private into public truth, but much more to do with how much of the truth should be told. Again, this might be justified in terms of protecting the practitioner against misuses of 'information'.

Such ethical considerations are quite independent from methodological ones, and must not be confused with considerations in which ethics are inextricably bound up with methodology. It is one thing to <u>negotiate</u> what the publicly accessible facts of a social situation are, and quite another to <u>negotiate</u> whether or not they ought to remain hidden. The confusion between these things in the minds of many democratic evaluators, including myself, has often I suspect sacrificed <u>the ethics of truth</u> for the <u>ethics of release</u>.

REFERENCES

Barnes J. A. (1977) <u>The Ethics of Inquiry in Social Science</u> Oxford University Press

Bonhoeffer D. (1949) 'What is Meant by Telling the Truth' in <u>Ethics</u> The Fontana Library, 1964

Brodbeck M. (1969) 'Meaning and Action' in <u>Readings in the Philosophy of the Social Sciences</u> ed. May Brodbeck, The Macmillan Co./Collier-Macmillan Ltd., London

Cupitt D. (1976) <u>The Leap of Reason</u> Sheldon Press

Habermas J. (1971) 'Techology and Science as "Ideology"' in <u>Toward a Rational Society</u> Heinemann, London

Hollis M. (1977) <u>Models of Man</u> Cambridge University Press

Hulmes E. (1979) <u>Commitment & Neutrality in Religious Education</u> Geoffrey Chapman, London

Chapter 3

HANDLING VALUE ISSUES

Michael Eraut

Introduction

Several theoretical, methodological and practical problems in handling value issues and negotiating evaluation goals are presented in this chapter. A divergent approach to evaluation is recommended which allows values external to a situation to be introduced alongside those of the participants, and which is appropriate in situations both of value conflict and of value complacency.

Value Transmission in Teaching and Evaluation

Whether teaching is regarded as a repressive or a subversive activity, it involves the transmission of values. Anyone who is not prepared for that responsibility should avoid becoming a teacher. But how far should a teacher be aware of the values he or she is responsible for transmitting? The answer, I would suggest, must depend on the extent to which these values are shared with other interested parties. If values are so embedded in the culture of a community that they are taken for granted by all its members, it is not the responsibility of a teacher working within that community to be uniquely aware of them. But if values are only shared by one section of the community, and the teacher is not aware of this, there is a problem. Such lack of awareness of values held by other sections of either the local community or the professional community is commonly found in evaluation studies. I call it value complacency. This complacency may sometimes be attributable to a particular group of teachers who 'choose' not to think about certain issues; or it may be the more general result of professional socialization. Some values are taken for granted in schools and teacher education, while others are treated as problematic; and it is open to debate whether the boundary has been appropriately drawn. However, whether value complacency is general to the education service or specific to a particular teacher or group of teachers, it raises problems for the evaluator.

A logical analysis suggests that a teacher may handle values in three different ways: (1) by assuming them or taking them for granted (implicit transmission); (2) by advocating them or refuting them and taking up a definite value position (explicit transmission); or (3) by making them the subject of his or her teaching with the intention of promoting pupils' value awareness while still preserving their autonomy (explicit discussion). Promoting value awareness as a teaching goal implies that values should be explicitly discussed but not imposed by the teacher, but this aim is difficult to achieve in practice. So we have to consider a further possibility, that of the unintentional transmission of values. Each of these four situations demands a different response from an evaluator. The first may signal value complacency. The second and third will often indicate value conflict - which values should be handled by transmission and which values by discussion? The fourth shows a failure to achieve intentions in a sensitive area.

The same analysis can also be applied to the evaluator's own activities. Both his actions during the evaluation and his final report may involve implicit, explicit or unintentional transmission of values. These values may come from participants in the evaluation, from sources external to the evaluation or from the evaluator himself. In this last case the values may derive either from the way the evaluation is conducted, i.e. they are built into the evaluator's role and procedures, or from personal views held by the evaluator.

Some of the principles suggested by this analysis will command general agreement among evaluators. For example, unintentional transmission of values by evaluators is undesirable though difficult to avoid in practice. Other principles may be more debatable. Can respect for evidence be treated as an assumed value? If value neutrality is claimed, should it be explicitly discussed? We might agree that an evaluator should avoid promulgating his personal values in the sense of explicit or implicit transmission; but would we agree that he should not introduce them for explicit discussion? I do not believe that these issues can be resolved by using facile labels like 'democratic' or 'bureaucratic', or by trying to oversimplify the complex web of influences, power relationships, rights and responsibilities that characterise our educational system. But I shall be returning to discuss some of these problems later. Here it is sufficient to note that ethical issues arise when an evaluator is confronted with value complacency as well as when he is confronted with value conflict.

The Goals of Evaluation

The idea of evaluation as a goal - oriented activity has been much neglected in recent British debates about methodology; and it also has a bearing on the much-debated distinction between evaluation and research. I do not wish to deny the importance of seeing evaluation as a process or discussing its principles of procedure; and I will be returning to this theme later on. But evaluations also have purposes and outcomes, and these too are relevant to the discussion of value issues. My own experience is largely in small-scale evaluation studies within single institutions where questions of purpose and outcome are unavoidable; and I am constantly surprised at their apparent neglect in large-scale public evaluations where goals often seem to be taken for granted. Though the analysis that follows is based on such small-scale studies, much of it may well be equally applicable to the others.

The first distinction I wish to make goes back to Scriven's classic paper "The Methodology of Evaluation" (Scriven 1967), but I hope to use less confusing terminology. What Scriven has called 'goals' and 'roles' I prefer to call intrinsic purposes and extrinsic purposes. Under intrinsic purposes I include both philosophic goals – estimations of worth, merit and value – and scientific goals – pursuit of truth, collection and presentation of data.[1] Under extrinsic I include goals such as accountability and guiding decision-making. Both types of purpose are present in all evaluations, interacting and making the tasks of the evaluator more difficult.[2] On the one hand the truth has to be pursued according to the criteria of the research community, while on the other the evaluator is expected to have some effect and this is judged according to the criteria of the practitioner community. Lack of resources will severely limit what can be done making it less probable that the evaluator will be able to fully satisfy either community. The evaluator has to choose what is to be done, and justify it in strategic as well as absolute terms given the resources available in the circumstances that existed at the time.

I find it useful to distinguish three main categories of intrinsic purpose: (1) examining the realisation of intention; (2) interpreting what is happening, and (3) ascribing value to actions, activities and programmes. Although all three categories will normally be present in an evaluation to at least some extent, their relative importance will vary. The first two are concerned with descriptive data, and hence include the elucidation and interpretation of values embedded within a programme or its context. The third concerns the value judgements that are or might be made about such a programme and about its intended or observed effects.

Values Embedded within a Programme

My first type of intrinsic purpose, examining the realisation of intention, includes the classical notion of assessing the achievement of objectives but is broader in conception. It does not assume that intentions are precisely formulated, that all participants have the same intentions or that intentions only relate to outcomes. There are many situations when intentions are conceived primarily in terms of participation, motivation and involvement; and it is assumed that beneficial outcomes will naturally follow.[3]

I shall focus primarily on problems associated with describing values that are implicit or explicit in the entity being evaluated; and this should not be taken as implying that other types of problem are any less significant when one is examining the realisation of intention. Beginning with observed values rather than intended values, I shall follow the Countenance model's (Stake, 1967) distinction between

Antecedents, Transactions and Outcomes. Observing values as outcomes is usually taken to mean assessing the extent to which pupils have come to hold certain values that the programme is intended to promote.[4] Methods of investigation include observation of pupil behaviour, interview and questionnaire -each with its attendant difficulties. One has to recognise that the validity of instruments purporting to measure values will always be rather limited, because there is a considerable gap between talk and action and betwen action in one context and action in another context. Moreover many intended value outcomes are long-term, with a time-span beyond that of most evaluation studies. Both these problems are found in moral education and social studies programmes. Other value outcomes are expressive rather than instructional (Eisner, 1969). For example a school may seek to promote artistic or recreational activities without being particularly concerned about which particular activities pupils eventually favour. Despite these problems, however, the question of values as outcomes is usually too important to be neglected. The evaluator has to make the most of the limited evidence at his disposal.

Observing values as antecedents presents similar methodological problems so I will not discuss it further. Again considerable caution is needed in interpreting the evidence. Indeed the difficulty of assessing what values people hold suggests that values can only be reliably observed when they are revealed by transactions. This perspective also accords with the notion that teachers do not often have specific objectives when communicating values because they are not sure what it is possible to achieve. When value goals are aspirations rather than expectations, the realisation of intention can be investigated only by examining the congruency of the observed transactions of a programme with what are often very long-term aims. The principal methods for collecting such evidence are direct observation and analysis of the material which teachers and pupils see, read and write; and the relationship between transactions and outcomes has to be argued logically rather than measured empirically.

Further problems arise when one seeks to determine what values are intended by teachers. Intentions can be uncertain or ambiguous and value awareness is often limited. Some intended values may be revealed in interviews, and others inferred from a teacher's behaviour or selection of material. But how about the values that are embedded in common forms of professional practice? Does the fact that the practice was intended necessarily imply that the values are also intended? When a teacher uses a book because it is 'good literature' does he necessarily intend that the values in it should be transmitted without question? One could hardly call his pupils' encounter with those values accidental. Issues such as these cannot be handled at the level of simple empirical description, they demand penetration beneath the surface; and this involves attempting to interpret what is happening.

I have used the phrase 'interpreting what is happening' to describe my second category of intrinsic purpose, because interpretation involves more than just finding out what is going on yet sounds less ambitious than explanation. Explanation in the scientific sense, i.e. as a result of conclusion-oriented inquiry (Cronbach and Suppes, 1969), is unlikely to result from an evaluation; but explanation in the historical sense of offering an interpretation of a complex array of causes and effect could well be a significant goal. To avoid explanation in this 'softer' sense is to deny that evaluation can have a formative role: and few people will be content to know that some of their intentions have not been realised without being given any indication of why this situation might have arisen (Cronbach, 1963; Hastings, 1966).

Focussing specifically on value issues two explanatory questions are of special interest. The first, 'Why is it that pupils receive some value messages more strongly than others?', has long been the preoccupation of writers on the 'hidden curriculum'. Dreeben (1968), Snyder (1971) and others have shown that outcomes directly contrary to a programme's expressed intentions may result from the dominant values of an organisation's social system or assessment system. Hence Parlett and Hamilton (1972) argue that evaluators must investigate the learning milieu as well as the instructional system. To ignore the wider context is to risk seriously misunderstanding what is happening.

A second question, 'How is it that some values come to influence a teacher more than other values?', is equally significant but less frequently asked. It involves trying to understand how conflicts of intention are resolved, and making the important distinction between intentions embedded in practice and the rhetoric of justification. Thus it is closely intertwined with the problem of discovering intentions which was raised a little earlier. The methodological difficulties of pursuing these questions are considerable, especially when techniques such as participant observation are ruled out by lack of time and opportunity. Hence I have been experimenting with a technique which I like to call 'instance interviewing'.

Instance interviewing involves basing an interview on the discussion of two or three instances.[5] It needs some object or some shared experience to provide a starting point, as questions about ordinary events are likely to be treated with suspicion or amazement. Day (1981) used video recordings of classroom events as a source of incidents. I have used student diaries and pupil exercise books. Such an interview can reveal factors affecting particular decisions and the way in which potential conflicts of value are resolved, by probing intentions in a context where the rhetoric of justification is inappropriate. The "theory of action" (Argyris and Schon, 1974) which is thus disclosed is largely tacit and implicit, taken for granted and embedded in personal practice. A more general interview, on the other hand, would be conducted in the language of 'talk about teaching' which has been carefully developed to preserve teachers' autonomy and to justify their actions. The linguistic difference can be seen by comparing the kind of teacher intentions revealed by Smith and Geoffrey (1968) with those of the recent Schools Council "Aims of Primary Education" Project (Ashton, 1975).

Value Judgements about a Programme

Hitherto we have been primarily concerned with descriptive data, with intended and observed values in the programme being evaluated and the problems of elucidating and explaining them. My third category of intrinsic purpose, value ascribing, is not so much concerned with values embedded within a programme as with value judgements about a programme. Again, I have found the debate about the handling of judgemental data somewhat impoverished, with little discussion of the validity problem or of how value issues should be treated in evaluation reports. There is even a tendency to ignore judgemental data altogether or to confine its collection to a narrow range of respondents. Indeed, the popular preference for formative rather than summative evaluation may be an attempt to escape from this kind of responsibility.

Perhaps the main reason for this retreat from discussing judgemental data has been a reaction to Scriven's (1969) declaration that:

His (the evaluator's) task is to try very hard to condense all that mass of data into one word: good or bad.

This overestimates what can be achieved with any reasonable degree of intellectual humility. Conflicting values cannot be 'condensed' without imposing some superordinate ethical framework. Few evaluators are prepared to accept this role of 'Philosopher king'. Still fewer believe it would be acceptable to others. But it is also recognised that the traditional positivist ideal of a scientific value-free evaluation is equally unattainable. Hence the notion of an evaluation report that finishes with a clear set of recommendations has been abandoned by many evaluators, although it is what many of their clients still expect. Such convergent evaluation can only be achieved by imposing values, either those of the evaluator or those of the people who commissioned him; or, in situations of value complacency, by some form of collusion between these two parties.

In Britain there have been two main responses to this dissatisfaction with convergent evaluation. One reaction has been the development of neutral evaluation, where the evaluator aims to be purely descriptive so that each of his audiences can draw their own independent conclusions, untrammelled by his own interpretations. It looks a useful recipe for conflict avoidance but I see three main drawbacks. First, data selection and interpretation are intimately connected processes so there is danger of unfocussed accounts embodying hidden principles of selection which preempt the possibility of independent interpretation. Second, such evaluations are inevitably rather lengthy and structureless so they are difficult to read, interpret and use. The evaluator saves his own conscience at the expense of not helping his clients. Third, I find the role of evaluator incompatible with that of pure empiricist, irrespective of whether he uses positivistic or naturalistic methods. Evaluation involves ethical as well as empirical enquiry almost by definition, and that is why I have emphasised its value ascribing purpose.

Illuminative evaluation has rather different aspirations, and its progressive focussing strategy leads to concise reports that are easy to read (Parlett and Hamilton, 1972). Its use of client-defined issues as a basis for selection is both practical and honest, but also brings disadvantages. It cannot import values which are not identified by the respondents, and this makes it of little use in situations of value complacency.[6] If one is concerned with what Habermas (1976) refers to as 'supressed interest' or what Lukes (1974) has called the 'third dimension of power', then one has to recognise that an evaluator may have an ethical responsibility to introduce values which have not been identified by the respondents. But can this be done in a manner which avoids imposing the evaluator's own personal views?

Divergent Evaluation

This section should be read rather differently from the rest of this paper as I am temporarily departing from my commentator role to explore an evaluation model which I have used with some success in small-scale evaluation studies and in the intrinsic analysis of curriculum materials (Eraut, 1975). I am not yet sure of its range of application, but it represents a constructive attempt to respond to some of the problems of handling judgemental data which we were discussing earlier. In particular, I find its ethical stance an attractive compromise between an evaluator's accountability to his immediate clients, his accountability to the wider public and his standards and values as a professional person working in education.

The process which I like to call divergent evaluation recognises that there are likely to be several different value positions and that some of them are potentially conflicting, and then attempts to relate the empirical evidence to these value positions without according priority to any of them. One of the tasks of the evaluator is to explore the connections between empirical evidence and the various values which might provide criteria for judging it. He thus places his ability to think and argue at the service of his different audiences as well as his ability to collect data. By showing linkages between the empirical evidence and certain values he is aiding those who espouse those values towards the judgements they are most likely to support: but since the same service is offered for rival values, all audiences are also reminded of the judgements that others are likely to make. This procedure also allows the evaluator to introduce values not heeded by any of his respondents without giving them any special priority. Thus divergent evaluation aims to increase sensitivity to other viewpoints, to represent all the value positions of involved parties, and to introduce additional values where appropriate.[7] Moreover, those who lose out on any final decision will find that their position has been treated with respect and that the evaluation has not been biased against them.

Some of the key questions which underpin this divergent approach to evaluation are as follows:

How is the programme viewed from divergent value positions?
By what criteria do people decide whether it is worthwhile?
Are there any additional criteria that it would be appropriate to introduce?
What arguments' could be used to justify or criticise the programme?
What value jugements and empirical judgements would these involve?
How well supported by evidence are the arguments?

Possible sources of additional values or criteria are the education literature, the views of people other than those consulted as participants, alternative forms of practice and the views of the evaluator.

Before moving on to look at some of the practical difficulties, let us explore the logic of evaluative argument a little further without claiming that people actually use the logic in practice. Arguments have to be justified as well as invented, and then logic does become important. When somebody makes a judgement about an educational programme, that judgement entails criteria or standards. The extent to which the programme meets each of these criteria is a separate empirical judgement, not necessarily independent because many criteria overlap. The selection and relative weighting of these criteria, however, is mainly a value judgement; though this too is not totally independent of some technical considerations.[8] Judgement is inherently complex, and I would argue that simply collecting people's judgements without seeking to explore their underlying structure is too narrow an approach for evaluators to readily adopt. It is closely analogous to confining empirical data-collection to the measurement of outcomes. It may indicate whether people approve of certain programmes but that is all.

In practice, few people make rational judgements in the logical way I have just described. The process is usually less deliberate, and people often have difficulty in explaining how they arrive at their judgements. They also tend to take 'shortcuts' by making judgements on one point on the basis of evidence that relates to quite a different point.[9] This need not prevent an evaluator from exploring some of the possible criteria being used: it just warns him not to assume that doing so will build up a rational coherent picture or a fair representation of someone's standpoint.

The opposite situation can be equally problematic. People do not necessarily hold coherent sets of values with clear priorities between them. They may not even hold fixed views on a particular educational programme. So it is often easier to explore possible components of a judgement without forcing people to decide on their relative weighting. That is why I am suspicious of many attitude questionnaires and opinion scales. Often they do not reveal judgements that have already been made but force people to make snap judgement there and then. However, their validity can be checked by interviewing a sample of respondents. Indeed I have found the interview follow-up of a questionnaire to be a valuable procedure, with the questionnaire providing a useful starting point for discussion. What difficulties did the respondent encounter filling it in? What did he think the question meant? Was it the right question to ask? Was he thinking of any particular incident. It becomes yet another approach to instance interviewing.

Another practical problem is the context and timing of any attempt to gather people's opinions on a course. The views expressed can be heavily influenced by the context in which the relevant questions are asked. For example, one of the interesting things I discovered when evaluating university science courses was that if you give students course evaluation questionnaires this immediately puts them in a 'mastery learning' frame of mind with the result that they show preference for a highly structured programme. However, if you talk to them about their degree course as a whole, their changes in attitude over the years, the place of academic work in university life and their career prospects, they are more likely to assume an 'intellectual development' frame of mind and show preferences for a weakly structured programme. The timing of an interview can be equally important. Consider talking to a teacher about the value of teaching multiplication tables by rote when any of the following events had occurred on the previous day. (1) An argument with an older colleague who teaches very formally about the handling of a child with behavioural problems; (2) a discussion with a probationer who does not believe in teaching tables at all, and who still has difficulty in keeping her class in order; (3) a parents' evening in a highly aspirant white-collar catchment area; (4) a test which showed her pupils performing badly in mechanical arithmetic; (5) an in-service course which examined children's misunderstanding of arithmetical processes; (6) a talk from a personnel officer from a large local firm, complaining of the standard of arithmetic shown by his apprentices. I hope you will forgive the stereotypes, but I think they make the point that the response is unlikely to be the same in each case.[10]

For all these reasons, I am prepared to argue a case for exploring components of value judgements rather than seeking final summary opinions. If the latter exist, they will soon be revealed; if they do not exist, why try and force them?. I would argue that people's selection of criteria and their empirical judgements on the basis of those criteria are likely to be more stable and reliable than their final judgements. The relative weighting of criteria is more likely to be influenced by context and timing, and forcing judgements in order to get hard data is likely to be counter-productive. Surely an evaluator hopes that people will suspend judgement until after they have read his report. So why encourage them to firm up their views in advance?

An alternative to the detailed mapping of separate criteria is to analyse judgemental data with the aid of Ideal Types. These are logically derived by empirically chosen, by a process which a colleague once described as a kind of naturalistic cluster analysis. Three stages are involved. (1) Values are explored in open interviews in order to establish the range of criteria used by the evaluator's audiences. (2) This evidence is used to construct three or four Ideal Types which encompass the full range of criteria, with each type being based in a position that emphasises a particular set of criteria to the virtual exclusion of all other. (3) The empirical evidence is examined from the standpoint of each Ideal Type in turn, and rival arguments about the merits of the course assembled. For example, when evaluating the curriculum of a Middle School I found that most of the relevant criteria could be derived from one of three ideal types – Integrated Day Man, Basic Skills Man and Traditional Subject Man. The arguments for and against the observed practice could then be presented from each of these three different viewpoints. This covered the full range of opinion without forcing any respondent to make a final summary judgement.

The advantages of this procedure are as follows:

1. Ideal Types are seen as extremes so everyone else becomes "a moderate".
2. Arguments can be presented sharply enough to be clearly understood and free of pretence (thus avoiding the current vogue for trying to say all things to all men and effectively saying nothing!).
3. The evaluation can be seen as unbiased, in the sense of not being based on one particular value position.
4. The whole range of opinion is catered for.
5. Nobody is placed in a position of having to defend some previously ascribed position.

The technique allows one to protect both confidentiality and divergency, and this is a considerable asset in situations of potential or actual conflict. But it is not universally applicable, and I have not always found it to be the most appropriate way of analysing judgemental data.

Extrinsic Purposes of Evaluation

The extrinsic purpose of an evaluation concerns the uses to which the information collected will be put; and again the situation is more complicated than many writers suggest. Consider, for example, the temporal aspect. All evaluations are of the past, in the present and for the future. Not only will most of the events being studied be past events, but even the evaluation itself will be a past event by the time it is concluded. The evaluation is "in the present" in the sense that if affects current events and is in turn affected by them, the interaction between the evaluator and the situation being evaluated can never be ignored. Then the most often quoted purpose of evaluation, namely "to guide decision-making", belongs in the future. Any actions taken as a result of an evaluation will be in the future and for the future. All three temporal elements are necessarily present but their respective importance may vary. For example, an emphasis on accountability will tend to concentrate on the past, an emphasis on contextual understanding or problem diagnosis will be primarily concerned with the present and an emphasis on decision-making will be oriented towards the future.

The dominant image of evaluation is still 'retributive', not primarily, I believe, because of lingering memories of 'payment by results' but because most evaluations are 'commissioned' by those 'in authority'. Hence those 'under authority' who are subjected to evaluation see themselves as potential victims (Elliott, 1978). They also suspect, with good cause, that information which reflects badly on their work will be more 'newsworthy' than information which reflect well -one of those facts of human life of which the popular press are only too well aware. Some evaluators try and escape their 'retributive' image by denying their link with the past and emphasizing that their sole purpose is to guide decisions in the future, but I personally do not believe that this attempt to sever the connection between evaluation and accountability is ethical. Most evaluations have an element of accountability in them somewhere, and it is dishonest to disguise it. Hence possible forms of reporting and access to information have to be discussed when arrangements about confidentiality are being negotiated.

The 'threat potential' of evaluation can be treated more constructively if one takes a more profesional view of accountability. Teaching is rarely a matter of total success or total failure and a competent professional will always fail to achieve some of his goals; so the grounds for external concern cannot just be that teachers are not wholly successful. Far more reprehensible, it might be argued, would be the failure to monitor one's teaching. However, even making a careful distinction between the evaluation of teaching and the evaluation of teachers does not resolve the problem of how to present negative information about teaching in a manner that is likely to have a constructive outcome. My usual response is to seek to legitimise the teaching by identifying it with some form of common professional practice, while at the same time making it abundantly clear that the teaching is not having the desired effect. The issue then ceases to be one of incompetence and becomes one of choosing the appropriate form of practice for the particular situation. This does not relieve the teachers concerned of any responsibility for taking action but it may prevent them from dismissing the evaluation as biased against them. For similar reasons I have always held the view that evaluative information about individuals should either by anonymous or remain confidential.

Our recent research into accountability has been exploring, among other goals, the implications of the general proposition that evaluation should be an integral part of normal professional conduct and that teachers should be held accountable for seeing that it was properly done. In particular, we found it useful to distinguish between general monitoring or trouble-shooting and long-term accountability for policies, performance and procedures (Becher, 1981). Monitoring is concerned with keeping things going by spotting any obvious signs of trouble and taking appropriate action. It usually takes existing policies and procedures for granted because its purpose would be defeated if it became too reflective or too time-consuming. Long-term accountability, on the other hand, would seem to imply some kind of programme of periodic reviews. These would not only be more systematic but more concerned with the appropriateness of policy and the general style of its implementation. The underlying question must be "Are we doing what is best?" and this inevitably involves judgements of value.

Unlike monitoring which is universal, reviews are relatively rare. Unavoidable decisions take precedence over avoidable decisions, regardless of their respective importance (Eraut, 1970). However, there is a growing view that school-based reviews are a professional responsibility that derives from the practice of delegating decisions to individual schools. Such reviews must involve at least some consideration of alternative policies and their respective merits and values (Eraut, 1978), if the question "Are we doing what is best?" is not to be totally ignored. But this suggests a need for teachers to be aware of different policy options and the values they entail. Hence I would argue that an evaluator participating in such a review has an obligation to develop option and value awareness.

Similar obligations arise when we consider the second extrinsic purpose of evaluation, that of guiding decision-making. It has become fashionable to claim to follow this goal as it conveniently avoids connotations of measurement or accountability. But what does it mean to take it seriously. At the very best careful consideration should be given to the precise nature of the decision which could follow the evaluation. Does one envisage course changes or minor improvements within a fixed curricular pattern, or is the pattern itself to be subjected to scrutiny? Will there be changes in aims as well as changes in the way the aims are being implemented? What range of policy options is likely to be examined? I have already argued that if there is a limited awareness of options it could be part of an evaluator's task to extend the range; and I would not like to add that he may need to collect evidence relevant to all the options being considered, and not just the existing state of affairs. The evidence relevant to untried options may be limited so this could involve visits to see how other approaches are working elsewhere. Such visits would not normally seek to collect performance data, as antecedent factors would render any direct comparison invalid. But they could reveal different value priorities, implementation problems and unexpected side-effects.

A third extrinsic purpose of evaluation is the development of contextual understanding. This goal is shared with organisational development and institutional research and cannot properly be considered as the only goal of an evaluation as opposed to a research study. But it could be an important subsidiary goal and often turns out to be more significant than was originally envisaged. Contextual understanding is important if one is seeking to predict the effect of proposed policy changes. It may also help people to improve the quality of their work within an existing policy framework; and it may help an organisation in a state of rapid change to keep some tabs on where it is going and what is happening to it. It is closely related to the intrinsic purpose of interpretation, the key distinction being that for extrinsic purposes the understanding needs to be shared by the participants and not confined to the evaluator and the research community.

Evaluation as problem diagnosis also belongs in this tradition, because its purpose is to get behind the symptoms and disclose the underlying factors. Though the need for speed and the atmosphere of crisis make this an unusually difficult and delicate task, the advantages of a short sharp investigation by a trained evaluator can be considerable. Not only should his experience prevent him from being immediately satisfied with the obvious explanation but he also has a potentially important role as a diplomat at a time when people's· ability to communicate with each other is usually rather low.

Negotiation of the Evaluation Brief

The emphasis which I have given to goals in this paper has been partly an attempt to redress the balance in response to current preoccupations with evaluator roles. But it also reflects a belief that goals need to be discussed much more; and I would argue that the relative priority to be given to the various intrinsic and extrinsic goals I have outlined should be part of the negotiation.

Earlier I drew attention to the inevitable influence of an evaluator on the situation he is studying. This influence is much greater than the well-known experimenter-effect in classical research designs, both because evaluation is more threatening than research and because an evaluator has a greater need to build good relationships. He needs not only co-operation but access to information as well. Thus evaluation cannot be considered as a purely intellectual process in which an evaluator plans his work, collects evidence about remote events and then reports. It is also a social process during the course of which people may feel threatened, annoyed, troubled, bored, concerned, interested, or even excited. How can an evaluator handle it? Does he attempt to maintain an aloof independence, or does he become involved? Who does he see as his clients?

Behind these questions lies a deeper issue - what is the source of authority in an evaluation? Apart from the question of who commissioned the evaluation with whose consent and under what conditions, there is the important question of generalisability.· The authority which an evaluator derives from membership of the research community relies on his access to generalisable knowledge and precise research techniques, whereas the authority of the participants derives research techniques, whereas the authority of the participants derives from their specialized knowledge of a particular context, expecially those aspects of it that are not readily described in terms of generalised knowledge and precise measurement. It would appear that the evaluator has to choose (1) precise measurement, independence, reliance on external authority and low access to contextual information, and (2) involvement, shared authority, reliance on situational validity and high access to contextual information.[11]

Each of these approaches has its disadvantages. The "independent" evaluator

-    has to rely on either authority or good salesmanship to gain co-

operation
- need to use relatively structured instruments
- appears remote and threatening
- gains little understanding of the context
- gets little interest in his report

whereas the "involved" evaluator

- gets drawn into disputes between client groups
- finds it difficult to criticise, or in any way to represent "the public interest"
- is liable to be accused of bias
- invests so much time in building and sustaining relationships that he has little left for other activities.

Moreover, while the "independent" evaluator is in danger of overemphasising his research role, the involved evaluator is in danger of ceasing to be an evaluator altogether and becoming a change-agent. Somewhere we have to find a balance.

I believe that the key to this problem of "independence versus involvement" lies in the notion of negotiated purpose and process; and I propose to base such negotiations on four main principles, two practical principles:

1. The evaluator will find it difficult to develop relationships and gain access to information without declaring his purpose and procedures; and a willingness to negotiate will usually improve his chances.
2. Increased participation in evaluation policy is likely to result in increased attention to evaluation results.

and two moral principles:

3. People have a right to know what an evaluator is doing and why.
4. All those who might reasonably be considered as clients have a right to some stake in the evaluation enterprise.

Let me suggest how I think this approach to evaluation as a social process might work in practice. After a brief period of familiarisation, the evaluator embarks on a fairly lengthy negotiation phase. First he asks his various client groups to contribute from their own perspectives to an initial agenda of issues, i.e. to say what they think the evaluation ought to be about. Secondly, he expands the agenda to include important issues that he feels have been omitted, and formulates it in a way that will allow new issues to emerge during the course of the evaluation. Thirdly, he uses the expanded agenda to negotiate agreement on the general purpose of the evaluation and invites comment on his proposed data-gathering procedures. Fourthly, he gets a promise of co-operation, and asks for additional help where he feels he can get it. For example, he may invite some of his clients to assist in the development and analysis of questionnaires - a process which brings them together in a situation where they can learn from each other, as well as involving them as "co-evaluators" - or to go through a file of student work and note the major difficulties and misunderstandings. I have tended to work fairly informally with only a short written agenda (about one side of a page), but in conflict situations greater formality may be necessary. Rippey (1973), for example, who describes evaluation studies of highly controversial urban education programmes, gives several cases where each rival client group has been invited to contribute items to a questionnaire and the detailed wording has been formally negotiated. He claims that this has not only helped to reduce the threat of evaluation but also helped client groups to develop more constructive relations with each other. At an individual level consultation over the agenda is a useful method for involving the type of client who leaves the evaluator to get on with it and then ignores the results if they displease him; while the "co-worker" approach provides a constructive role for clients who wish to vet every move the evaluator makes.

Conclusion

This paper has been an attempt to explore a large number of both theoretical and practical problems associated with the handling of value issues in evaluation studies. The goal analysis has helped to give it coherence but should not be regarded as authoritative. Nor should the occasional digressions to consider personal approaches to the solution of methodological problems. The paper is intended to be exploratory and I hope people will read it and discuss it in that frame of mind. If at times my position seems a little firmer than it really is, that is because I have tried to be constructive. Being constructive is part of my ethical stance as an evaluator; and, however difficult the problems under discussion, I would not want this paper to contradict that message.

NOTES

1. I would argue that this and following statements have meaning without assuming a positivistic role for social science, an absolutist approach to values or an objectivist attitude to truth!
2. I also recognise that the distinction between intrinsic purpose and extrinsic purpose is not absolute. Habermas for example would claim that truth is not unrelated to utility. However the distinction draws attention to likely areas of conflict and I find it a useful aid to thinking about evaluation strategy.
3. Stake (1967) provides a useful framework for examining the realisation of intention in the descriptive half of his Countenance of Evaluation Model, though one has to recognise that the distinction between a transaction and an outcome may depend on the level of analysis. For example, if a film is shown and written about for homework, that homework would be an outcome if one was evaluating the lesson or the film but a transaction if one was evaluating the whole course.

4. Assessing whether the pupils value the programme, i.e. their attitude towards it, would be collecting judgemental rather than descriptive data; and is therefore discussed later. However it must be acknowledged that value outcomes and judgements cannot be entirely separated.

5. The method bears some resemblance to Flanagan's (1954) Critical Incident Technique, but seeks to focus on typical incidents at least as much as critical incidents.

6. A somewhat similar point, but without this specifically ethical dimension is made by Parsons (1976).

7. The argument here is that in so far as evaluation is concerned with the pursuit of truth, there is an obligation for an evaluator to help people see values as problematic. Making them aware of other people's values may help, even when those other people are not immediate participants. It also reduces the likelihood of the evaluator himself unconsciously adopting the values of one particular group.

8. Some values may turn out to be commonsense beliefs that can be empirically tested. But such testing is rarely feasible within an evaluation study and the research literature suggests that it would only rarely lead to a conclusive outcome. So while such beliefs can be clearly labelled as empirical they have to be treated almost as if they were value judgements.

9. The well-known "halo" effect by which judgements of goodness (or badness) get over-generalised is but one example of this phenomenon.

10. On our recent accountability study we found that the context of meetings and their timing with respect to press reports on sensitive issues caused considerable variation in teacher opinion. So also did a period of industrial action.

11. There is, of course, a socio-anthropological research tradition which involves both unstructured techniques and independence, but I do not believe this position could be sustained by anyone formally labelled as an "evaluator".

REFERENCES

Argyris C and Schon D (1974) Theory in practice: increasing professional effectiveness Jossey-Bass

Ashton P et al (1975) Aims into practice in the primary school University of London Press

Becher T Eraut M and Knight J (1981) Policies for Educational Accountability Heineman

Cronback L (1963) Course Improvement through Evaluation Teachers College Record 64 (8) 672-83

Cronback L and Suppes P (eds) (1969) Research for Tomorrow's Schools: Disciplined Inquiry for Education Macmillan New York

Day C (1981) Classroom Based In-Service Education: the development and evaluation of a client centred model Occasional Paper 9 University of Sussex

Dreeben R (1968) On what is learned in school Addison - Wesley

Eisner E (1969) 'Instructional and expressive educational objectives: their formulation and use in curriculum' in W J Popham (Ed) Instructional Objectives AERA Curriculum Evaluation Monograph 3 Rand McNally

Elliott J (1978) 'Classroom Accountability and the Self Monitoring Teacher' in W Harlem (Ed) Evaluation and the Teacher's Role Macmillan

Eraut M (1970) 'The role of evaluation' in G Taylor (ed) The Teacher as Manager Councils and Education Press

Eraut M Goad L and Smith G (1975) The Analysis of Curriculum Materials Occasional Paper 2 Education Area University of Sussex

Eraut M (1978) 'Accountability at school level' in T Becher and S Maclure (Eds) Accountability in Education N.F.E.R. Publications

Flanagan (1954) 'The critical incident technique' Psychological Bulletin Vol 51 pp 327-58

Habermas J (1978) Legitimation Crisis Heinemann

Hastings T (1966) 'Curriculum Evaluation: The Why of the Outcomes', Journal of Educational Measurement Vol 3 pp 27-32

Lukes S (1974) Power Macmillan London

Parlett M and Hamilton D (1972) Evaluation as illumination: a new approach to the study of innovatory programmes Occasional Paper 9 Centre for Research in the Educational Sciences University of Edinburgh

Parsons C (1976) 'The New Evaluation: a cautionary note' Journal of Curriculum Studies Vol 8 No 2

Rippey R N (ed) (1973) Transactional Evaluation McCutchan

Scriven M (1967) 'The Methodology of Evaluation' in R W Tyler R M Gagne and M Scriven Perspectives of Curriculum Evaluation AERA Curriculum Evaluation Monograph I Rand McNally

Scriven M (1969) 'Evaluating educational programs' Urban Review Vol 3 pp 20-22

Smith L M and Geoffrey W (1968) The Complexities of an Urban Classroom Holt/Rinehart/Winston

Snyder B R (1971) The Hidden Curriculum Knopf

Stake R E (1967): 'The Countenance of Educational Evaluation' Teachers College Record 68 523-540

Chapter 4

UNDERSTUDY - EVALUATOR SEEKS AUTHORS TO DISCUSS
ETHICS

Clem Adelman

Introduction

In Great Britain from 1962 until 1972 the numbers of students
preparing to become teachers doubled, reaching 120,000 in the
Colleges of Education and Polytechnics alone. This increase was
required in order to meet the increasing numbers of schoolchildren,
the modest reduction in the size of school classes, the raising of the
school leaving age from 15 to 16 and the increasing numbers of pupils
staying on past 16 years of age. Much of the responsibility for the
'supply' of additional teachers was handed over to the colleges of
education; institutions that, although fiscally under the control of
local authorities, were at that time, academically under the aegis of
universities. The debates about the quality of teacher preparation and
practices culminated in the commissioning of a committee to look into
and make recommendations about teacher training. The committee
under Lord James reported in December 1971.

The Report (Jan. 1972) omitted the text of a final chapter on the
consequences of the impending fall in the birth rate. The news of this
decrease, as with most demographic statistics, was slow to emerge,
taking two years in this instance. This decrease of 6% per annum in
the birth rate had commenced in 1968. Although the consequences for
the colleges of education were known and discussed in the deleted
chapter, no member of the James Committee could make public this
information. Members of this Committee, as with all committees
commissioned by a government, are sworn to secrecy.

In December 1972, the first indications that there would be
major consequences for the colleges of education as a result of the
decrease in the birth rate, were included in the ironically titled
Department of Education and Science White Paper Education: a
Framework for Expansion. Lightly, politely, and usually as a tailpiece
to a section, the message came through that expansion would cease,
and under certain circumstances, reduction and even closure of
colleges, could occur. Both the James Report and the White Paper
suggested that colleges of education in general, might devise and offer
additional programmes of study. These programmes would be of a

43

different content and have different purposes to those directed to the preparation of teachers. This expansion in the range of the curriculum became known as 'diversification'. Subsequent Department of Education and Science circulars suggested that diversification in these colleges of between 1,000 to 2,000 might best be achieved through a course arrangement based on unit or modular components. Provision, it was recommended, should be made for those who were unsure of whether they wish to become teachers (the numbers involved were unknown).

At the end of "Framework for Expansion" the question was posed as to whether, through diversification and amalgamation with colleges of technology, the emergent curriculum would become indistinguishable from that of the polytechnics. Thirty polytechincs had been commissioned in 1966 to promote the application of technology and arts. In the context of a smaller population of 18 year olds, such claimed "duplication of function" was wasteful, in the view of the government.

At the point of least momentum, just before the rising wave of expansion crashed on the unknown shores of contraction, a minority of colleges of education began to devise new programmes of study - to diversify. One of these colleges, whose principal had been a member of the James Committee, was confident in its ability to develop a diversified curriculum. The Principal had, along with a few senior staff, become interested in evaluation, particularly of the "illuminative" type, that would "inform policy makers". Alongside this was an interest in the possibilities of institutional self-study. On the initiative of the Principal drafts of a proposal which, if funded, would enable the colleges to engage in such self-study, were written. Consultations with members of Her Majesty's Inspectorate, established persons in research and evaluation in Great Britain and abroad, brought forth a proposal to the Department of Education and Science.

The DES suggested a comparative study of three institutions undergoing diversification; instead of a case study of one institution, the intention was to allow for some 'generalised findings' to emerge. 'Institutional self-study' was considered too narcissistic by the DES. Public funds could not be seen to be spent to assist the development of one college whilst others were equally deserving.

The DES was also concerned about the educational consequences of introducing a unit or modular based degree course, as such arrangements were relatively untried in Great Britain. The study was to collect information about how such course arrangements operate to enhance "student choice" and give the option of a delay in a decision about whether to prepare to become a teacher.

The final proposal to DES continued to incorporate a multiplicity of other topics on which information was to be collected, reflecting the different interests of consultants, DES representatives and some senior members of the colleges.

The collection and analysis of student admissions and achievement statistics was required. Considerable store was put on information already collected since 1973 about the student intake, their qualifications and selection of courses, and so on, as evidence of potential productivity of the study.

Leading academics, in particular those with an interest in evaluation, were asked to suggest possible candidates for the position of principal investigator. Letters drawing attention to the national advertisements and inviting application were distributed to recommended candidates, there were serious misgivings amongst prospective investigators about the requirement that investigators be resident in an institution that they were evaluating. However, the project had been agreed to by the DES although the formal research proposal, which was to be the task of the principal research investigator upon appointment, had not been submitted. Presumably it was considered that the writing of this proposal was an aspect of 'academic freedom'.

Although there was some uncertainty in the colleges of education about their future numbers of students, it was the scale of the cuts (student numbers were to be reduced by two-thirds within five years) that came as a shock to the colleges. The publication of the DES decision and its announcement to the College came two months after the principal investigator had commenced work. The "stability" upon which self-study had been premised seemed to disappear - the spectres of reorganisation, staff redundancies, and even closure, if students could not be found for the rapidly expanding range of diversified programmes, loomed.

A steering committee had been established just prior to the appointment of the principal investigator. The membership of this committee was decided by the college in consultation with some academics. DES representatives were ex officio members. This steering committee, as will be illustrated later, was one of the major pre-conditional constraints on the autonomy of the evaluators.

Methodology and Evaluation

Although evaluators of education programmes and projects have developed a wide range of methodologies and are generally concerned with social values and epistemology, few educational evaluators have made explicit or public any worry about necessary conditions for the application of their methodologies.

The evaluation proposition tends to be: if methodology X is used, then the following consequences are likely to ensue. The full proposition should read: if methodology X is used, under these conditions, then these consequences are likely to ensue. Some conditions for the conduct of evaluation are set prior to the commencement of the evaluator's work; they are preconditions, although the evaluator's awareness of these preconditions may not emerge until some time after the evaluator has commenced work.

Although alternatives to pre-test, post-test types of evaluations have been developed, notably by Stake (1975), Scriven (1967), Eisner (1967) and McDonald (1976), even these workers have made few explicit statements concerning such pre-conditions although they have written about procedures of evaluation.

The Evaluation

Taking seriously the aspiration towards institutional self-study yet realising the delicacy of public comparison of three institutions in the process of such an enterprise, with reports going to the agency that not only funded the project but also maintains considerable control over the institutions, this evaluator declared himself 'independent'. 'Independent' was meant to convey the intention to remain free from the commissions and commands of the senior administration in the three colleges, any factions of the three colleges, and of the Department of Education and Science.

I did not wish to avoid social contacts; on the contrary, arising from a sympathy with the fieldwork methods of social anthropology, such contacts were seen as of primary importance. Rapport had to be established but, on the other hand, co-option into factions was to be avoided.

The staff tended to treat the evaluators in residence as ordinary members of the institution, making no comment on the declaration of independence.

The majority of individuals within the colleges with whom I came in contact had at least some understanding that I was not a regular member of the institution (I did not teach, invigilate, assess and so on), nor, accordingly, was I subject to the same schedules or incorporated within the formal organisation of the institution. However, such independence was a source of discomfort to some members of the institution in which the research project ("SCIC") was based.

No particular member of the institutions was to have privileged access to project information, all members of the institution would have the right to negotiate access; and if that access were agreed, then that information would be made public (i.e. distributed). However, the contractual requirement that information about institutions be reported to the Steering Committee, on which the DES representatives sat, rested uneasily with the assurances of the evaluators that they were independent. The succession of cut-backs in student quota numbers, redundancies and limits on staffing, combined to produce a climate of anxiety and scepticism which was not conducive to an enterprise such as institutional self-study. In spite of initial declarations to be independent evaluators, these declarations were not significant to staff and had to be restated throughout the project.

Although the 'academic freedom' and the conduct and design of the project were specifically assigned to the research workers, the preordinate proposals and contract required not only data to be made available to the DES Statistical Unit "within the usual safeguards of anonymity", but the DES regarded themselves as the priority audience. Their main interest was by now quite clear: to collect statistics and other information from the research workers, who would report back to them.

The DES permanent civil servant considered that a study funded by the DES should adhere to the propositions of the original proposal. As the DES had funded the study, they assumed the right to require that the enquiry followed these original specifications. Her Majesty's Inspectors' representatives, however, were more concerned about allowing the project to maintain its 'academic freedom' and to develop according to the sort of information that was being collected, although adhering to a considerable extent to the 'spirit' of the original proposal. Although the original funding initiative had come from the HMI's, the formal responsibility for the project was with the Planning and Research section of the DES under the control of the permanent civil servants. This shift in responsibility for the project was significant. The interest of Her Majesty's Inspectors in the institutional development aspects of the study was of little interest to the Planning and Research Section which had an avowed positivistic approach to research. They proceed by commissioning research to their own a priori specifications and expect 'proof' or refutation of their initial propositions, along with predictive statistics.

The Steering Committee

During two meetings of the Steering Committee, one after eight months and another after eighteen months, the question of extent to which the project's work had adhered to the original itemised collection of information arose. At the later Steering Committee the DES representatives asked to be included in confidentiality arrangements that had been established between the three colleges.

The DES were concerned that the hierarchical control of research within universities should be applicable in the case of this project. It was through the Steering Committee that they applied pressure on the research workers to conform with the original propositions of the project and to address their work to particular topics and exclude others (such as social class of the student intake, the influence of validating bodies on curriculum, the process of institutional change and adjustment). As the DES pointed out at a Steering Committee meeting, the conditions of control of research with a university are that a Professor is accountable to the funding agency for the progress and completion of the project. In the case of SCIC, although the title 'Research Director' was nominally designated by the DES, it was specified that this would be restricted to project management especially of the finances of the project. As was pointed out by one of the university professors on the Steering Committee, the 'project director's' job was analogous to that of the Bursar rather than a Professor within a university.

The Steering Committee was not, as it described itself in initial meetings, purely for 'advice and discussion' of reports. The one member of the Steering Committee who had no vested interests was the most forthright in his advice and discussion. The other members, knowing the influence of the DES on the uncertainties of the future, protected their own interests through mutual avoidance of the mention of or commentaries on sensitive issues raised by the research reports.

Barriers to the Feedback and Use of Evaluation/Research Reports

Although many of the evaluators' reports to the Steering Committee incorporated details of academic organisation, course arrangements, course uptake, enrolment, withdrawals, and avoided the release of descriptive and very specific reports, the interpretations, although tending to be bland, still could be objected to by individual colleges, especially where comparison between the three colleges was cited.

Establishing a responsive audience

The Steering Committee was not a condusive forum for frank discussion. Nor were the colleges. The colleges, it was discovered, had not preceded the commencement of the project with any public discussion of the purposes of the project. They had no experience of using evaluation information or anything but basic registry statistics in their planning and policy.

Whereas those who have studied and who have attempted to bring about institutional change recommend the use of change agents, such intermediaries who would utilize the information provided were not a precondition of the project. (W. F. Whyte, 1965) (Benn, et al 1976). The three predetermined 'link-men' between the research workers and the colleges were, as members of the institutions, bound to act within the institution's own organisational and communication channels. Although they were senior members of the institutions, the final authority was that of Principal or Director of the institution. When it became clear that the link-men were obviously incapable of disseminating information in a way appropriate to bring about corporate institutional self-study, Discussion groups were set up in each college. No member of the Discussion group took responsibility for the further dissemination of any of the information, although they could recommend that documents be made available more widely. The research workers declined to engage in the active dissemination of their information, although in informal circumstances they discussed ideas with interested members of staff. By inserting a point of view, even if based on empirical evidence, the evaluators found that they either became enmeshed in the politics and value conflicts within the institutions and were inevitably sided with by some and opposed by others, and thus entered the politics of the institutions.

More often, the evaluation reports were ignored on the basis that the 'research workers' were not members of the institution; that institutional policy making and decision were within the ambit of the politics of the institution and could only be engaged in by institutional members.

The audience for the research reports became restricted to those interested members within the institutions. These Discussion groups enabled the researchers to test the pertinence of the issues they were investigating and the significance of the information they collected as reported to each of the colleges.

The discussion groups had been set up in the three colleges in October 1977 in response to a suggestion by the project team during a Steering Committee meeting. However, the differing means of control over information within the three institutions led to the discussion groups being of quite different composition. In one institution the discussion group comprised senior staff appointed by the principal; in another, the group was based upon an a priori seminar convened by the principal, which included both senior and other staff. In the third institution an invitation was extended to all staff by the principal. The principal, although receiving documents, declined membership of the group.

Preconditions

Some preconditions for the research were known by the evaluators. These included the broad intentions of the project and the staffing, and the putative 'academic freedom' for the design and accomplishment of the enterprise, and the duration and resources of the project. But the major preconditions only began to be known after SCIC commenced. These included:

1. The nature of the negotiations which brought in the other two colleges and the sort of agreements that were made with them.
2. The expectation that the research workers be included within a part of the college organisation and advise and be consulted on matters not only concerned with the project, but in other areas of their expertise.
3. The requirement that unspecified data be handed over to the DES Statistics Section. The appearance of the methodology upon which the DES had agreed to study emerged eight months after the project had commenced, and one year after the initial 'frank' appointment interviews.
4. The vested interests of the Steering Committee - the nature of discussions could not be predicted with certainty from these vested interests.
5. The DES's influence on the project - trying to hold the researchers to the original proposal upon which the money had been granted, rather than to incorporate self-study.
6. That the evaluators might teach, supervise dissertations and act on commissions from senior staff.

As the contract had been devised prior to the arrival of the evaluators and funded by a government agency, there was little point in suggesting that a rolling contract be arranged which would take into account the exigencies of the change of circumstances and the appropriateness of the original proposal. Although sceptical and suspicious, they could not know that crucial preconditions had been withheld from them and could not, as with a rolling contract, explicity revise their schedules.

Only through fortuitous meetings within the social network of people who had been consulted prior to the project, both in Great Britain and abroad, and by accounts of the project given by some informed members of the institutions who were not within the senior administration, could these suspicions about the preconditions be confirmed as founded rather than paranoid.

The difficulties of the project had been expressed during discussions with members of the research and evaluation workers.

Although their initial understanding of the evaluation had been that it was routine and concerned with students' satisfaction and staff self-esteem the discussions revealed the extent to which the project was revealing the way in which institutions operated. The catching up of the evaluation into unforeseen politics made the project of more interest and more significance to other evaluators. To have resigned early on, for instance after the Steering Committee meeting eight months after the project had commenced, after undisclosed preconditions had been revealed, might have been seen as an honourable thing to be a subject discipline-based researcher, but not by evaluators interested in the politics of evaluation.

Some Intermim Conclusions
    The evaluators had aspired to conduct a 'responsive' evaluation (Stake, 1975). The appropriateness of such an evaluation was premised on information that was made available to the evaluators, responses to the preliminary questions asked by the evaluators and the assurances given. The actuality was one of pre-emptive specification by the DES with regard to the collection of data; of expectations by the institutions, especially by the institution in which the researchers were resident, to act as active change agents willing to be co-opted into the activities within that college in particular. By maintaining independence from the commissions and commands and from factions within the college, and by declining co-option, the evaluators were in a position of maximum advantage in terms of access to information in that, not being enmeshed in the beliefs and values of the institution and yet by being available within the institution to all members, they could engender rapport and gain an overview of the institution that no other member of the institution had privilege to. Not only was there information about the internal workings of one institution, but to a lesser extent about the internal workings of two other institutions. However, although knowing much, and understanding some, did not make it any easier to release information within the institutions as any sensitive information had political consequences, especially in the context of possible closure of one of the institutions, staff cut-backs, the 'vendetta principle', (Ostregren, 1978) and the suspicion that the researchers might be working directly on behalf of the DES or the senior administration. If they had been visiting evaluators they would have had the benefit of being able to write reports and not have to face every day the consequences of meeting people who had been affected by this, and in addition would have had a group of researchers and evaluators with whom to discuss any problems that were arising and to compare notes.

Towards a reconceptualisation of the evaluator's dilemmas
    I consider that there is a vital connection between the independence of the evaluator and the conduct of evaluation. The nature of the institution or programme, or system, as already established prior to the commencement of the evaluation, has been identified as one precondition. The other preconditions relate to the nature of the contract drawn up between the evaluator and the funding

agency. The funding agency may or may not be identical to that which funds the programme, institution or system. It is more likely that, if the evaluation has a separate funding agency, the evaluator might be able to negotiate independence as a precondition. In contrast to a negotiated independence, the funding agency may require the evaluator to contract into a pre-specified brief. Other preconditions are: whether the evaluator is to be visiting or resident within the institution, programme or system and whether the evaluator is to receive salary from the funding agency or from the programme, institution or system which is being evaluated. In most cases, funded evaluation has been external, although where the evaluation funding agency is identical with that which funds the insitutional system the credibility for such externality becomes difficult to maintain.

These preconditions form part of the <u>first contract</u> which is negotiated prior to the fieldwork stage of the evaluator's work. The <u>second contract</u> concerns the relationships established by the evaluator with those to be studied. This second contract involves the procedures for the conduct of the evaluation. The essential dimension here is that of <u>independence</u> from collusion with interest groups within the institution, programme or system, in contrast to <u>co-option</u> or collusion with such interest groups.

For fieldworking evaluators there is inevitably some tension between these dimensions, and for those who work by participant observation and interviewing there is a delicate boundary between getting to know the values, beliefs and norms of the different factions and becoming involved in, or identified with, these factions. This delicate boundary becomes confused when the evaluator simultaneously engages in action research or development. Such confusion tends to be reduced if the evaluator is working for himself and those being studied. But it is unusual for funding agencies to be so altruistic.

The second, subsequent contracts are premised on the nature of the first contract. For the evaluator to ignore the first contract is to self-assign power, in societies where evaluators can only have influence. This second contract involves the communication of the project's intentions to those to be studied, establishing communication channels for access, release and distribution of evaluation documents, and assigning the responsibility for such release and distribution, and establishing to whom particular sorts of documentation might be released, along with any confidentiality agreements and rights of ownership of evaluation information.

<u>Some types of Evaluation Procedure and Preconditions</u>

Type 1:   Autonomy
            External/visiting
            Independent

this is the type of evaluation that most evaluators desire, and some achieve. The evaluation has considerable credibility and is seen as being fair and 'objective'.

Type 2:   Pre-specified brief
           Internal
           Resident co-opted

this type of evaluation the evaluators are considered as 'bought' by
those in power. It has little credibility, adding to technical control
suggestive of alternative means and a diversity of interests.

Type 3.   Pre-specified brief
           External
           Resident independent? or co-opted?

This type seems to apply to quango/research employment agencies
which are given a pre-specified brief by their paymasters, transmit
this   pre-specified   brief   that   the   agency   employs   as
evaluators/researchers;   places the evaluators into residence in the
institution's programmes and systems to be studied, accepting that
these evaluators will retain high allegiance to the pre-specified brief.
    If the evaluators find during their field-work that the pre-
specified brief has little relationship, or is what they consider to be
distorted, or contains unfair premises in the light of their field-work,
the evaluators/researchers then tend to side with those being studied,
although not necessarily all the factions amongst those being studied.
The evaluator then becomes the spokesperson (Schensul, 1980) for
those studied, perhaps in opposition to the premises of the pre-
specified brief. If a group of evaluators come to similar conclusions,
then the research agency or quango has considerable problems in
trying to explain the findings of the evaluation and the conduct of the
evaluators to its paymasters.
    If autonomy can be negotiated, then it may also be possible to
negotiate mutual-culpability for all those involved in the evaluation.
When the evaluators' reports find that the premises of the evaluation
are inadequate or inaccurate, or what has been studied is indicating
such marked change or adjustment, the evaluators' work becomes
extremely difficult to carry through in the light of the premises of the
original contract. Then such mutual culpability can lead to a revised
contract with the evaluators. Such mutual culpability has to take in
the funding agency as well as the evaluator and those to be studied,
and any other influential or powerful interest group. A succession of
revised contracts – the rolling contract – may become the evaluator's
procedure for maintaining not only his credibility but also his
reputation.
    It would be clear to the reader by now that I am suggesting that
the fundamental differences between what have been distinguished as
different types of evaluation are to found at the level of preconditions and procedures. Distinctions at the level of methodology
and techniques, such as 'illuminative' (Parlett, M. and Hamilton, D.
1977) and 'goal-free' (Scriven, 1972), are premised on particular
preconditions and procedures. It is unfortunate that, apart from a few
exceptions, evaluators have not been explicit about preconditions and
procedures but have concentrated on differences in methodology and

techniques. Novice evaluators and those who synthesize the literature on evaluation have attended more to the aspects of evaluation that are similar or identical with those used in social research and less to the distinguishing features of evaluation-preconditions and procedures. Popham (1975) suggests that "Education evaluators must realise that their expertise is no substitute for tactful interaction with those around them. Evaluators who walk into an educational setting and expect deferential treatment merely because they know omega squared, are in for a surprise". But even if "tactful interaction" is fulfilled, the endeavour of evaluation is dependent on the nature of the contract, target audiences, the extent of influence of the funding agency and prior assumptions of the process by which the means of the evaluation might be achieved.

Concluding Remarks

I believe that evaluators should attend to preconditions and procedures as much as they attend to methodology. Having tried to describe the conflicts and confusions of an evaluation where the evaluators' efforts were often pre-empted by preconditions that were not made explicit before the evaluators were employed, I would want to precede employment as an evaluator by firstly clarifying these questions:

a) Who am I working for?
b) Who and how was it decided that the problem was worth proposing and funding?
c) What arrangements and expectations have preceded the bringing in of the evaluators?
d) Who are the audience(s)?
e) Would the evaluator be required to relinquish some autonomy over the conduct of the evaluation?
f) To what extent might the evaluator specify conditions on the release and particularise the use of evaluation reports?

Evaluators have often assumed that all preconditons had been made explicit to them during the negotiation of the evaluation contact. Any subsequent preconditions would form part of the evaluation and possibly form constraints or freedoms within a rolling contract.

In the case of the SCIC evaluation information was withheld (whether deliberately or not) which would have enabled those responsible for the evaluation to have made more informed decisions about the methodology and procedures. It was a project about gate-keepers across the communication channels within the colleges; it was about pre-emptive propositions which became inappropriate in changed circumstances; it was about what happens when the funding agency also controls the institutions about which the research is reporting. Although evaluators (and researchers) may have little control over how their information is used, I am convinced that evaluators and researchers in the social world should be given all the information that pertains to the proposed project in order that they may make a decision as to whether to become involved. This decision is as much ethical as methodological. (It may be that this description of the nature of the control over the evaluation is unfair to the persons and parties concerned as they may not have been able to envisage the consequences of their joint actions and interactions).

It seems to me that there are warnings within this project for evaluators in general. If the circumstances are ones of change, then the contract should be a rolling contract; if the information might affect all members of the institution, then it seems to me to be up to the institutions to negotiate within their own structures and within their own politics they way in which such a project would proceed, and these deliberations would form part of the negotiation of the contract. Evaluators should not be placed in undisclosed cross-fire of a preconditional conflict between a funding agency and the proposers of the project.

REFERENCES

Benn, K., Bennis, W.G., and Chinn, R. (1976) in "The Planning of Change". Holt, Reinhardt, Winston, 2nd edition.

Department of Education and Science (1972) Education: A Framework for Expansion. H.M.S.O., London.

Department of Education and Science (1972) Teacher Education and Training. (James Report) H.M.S.O., London.

McDonald, B. (1976) 'Evaluation and the Control of Education' in Safari I, Centre for Applied Research in Education, University of East Anglia, Norwich.

Ostergren B. (1978) 'The Swedish Project on Institutional Self-evaluation', paper presented at the OECD-IMHE Conference on Institutional Management in Higher Education, September 12, 1978. Paris. "A particularly difficult case of decision-making is to reallocate resources by reducing or even eliminating existing programs in order to start new activities. And such a reallocation is extremely difficult to achieve in an academic system, because the forces balance each other in accordance with the vendetta principle: if you put your knife in me (or my discipline, or my department, or my students) today, I will put my knife in your (your discipline, department, students) tomorrow - so let us not use our knives. And so status quo is preserved".

Parlett, M. and Hamilton, D. (1977). 'Evaluation as illumination: a new approach to the study of innovatory programmes' in D. Hamilton et al Beyond the Numbrs Game, London, Macmillan.

Popham, W. (1975) 'Educational Evaluation', Prentice Hall, New Jersey.

Scriven, M. (1967) 'The Methodology of Evaluation' in AERA Monograph 1 on Curriculum Evaluation. Rand McNally & Co., Chicago.

Scriven, M. in De. Hamilton et al. (1977) 'Beyond the Numbers Game', in Macmillan. Especially pp 132, 134-138.

Stake, E. (1975) "Responsive Evaluation" In: Evaluating the Arts in Education. Merrill, Ohio.

Whyte, W.F. and Hamilton, E. (1965) Action Research for 'Evaluating the Arts in Education'. Merrill, Ohio.

Whyte, W.F. and Hamilton, E. (1965) 'Action Research for Management'. Irwin Dorsey, Illinois.

Chapter 5

NEGOTIATING CONDITIONS FOR INDEPENDENT EVALUATIONS

Helen Simons

Introduction

Ten years ago it might have been presumed that all evaluations in accordance with the conventions and canons of responsible impartial reporting in research were independent in the conduct of their inquiry and dissemination of their products. Now there seems to be a need to establish the case. This chapter addresses this central theme – that there is a need to negotiate appropriate conditions to ensure independence of evaluations in the conduct of the inquiry by reporting accurately and fairly all the different value positions of participants in the programme; and in the dissemination of the product/s of the evaluation to all those who have a right to knowledge about the programme.

Essentially the chapter raises three points. The first is that evaluation practice has become subject to more and more contractual controls and interventions, not to mention censorship. Conflicts have arisen to the point where participants -whether they be teachers, managers, sponsors or evaluator/s have threatened or sought legal advice.

The second point is that the tradition of informality in this country which seems to promote freedom of operation for the evaluator actually results in much greater evaluator vulnerability to controlling pressures from those who have more power in the system.

Thirdly I argue that the evaluator should take the initiative in articulating the kinds of agreements and conditions that are necessary to secure independent evaluations or this initiative may be taken by those less informed about the conditions necessary for worthwhile inquiry.

The potentialities and problems associated with written agreements are discussed and too legal an analogy dismissed as being counterproductive to the social process of conducting evaluations and making results accessible. Negotiation of conditions and resolution of difficulties, it is argues, are best achieved through dialogue than through recourse to the law.

Finally I suggest some rules of thumb which may prove helpful in thinking about how to formulate agreements for the conduct, outcomes and dissemination of independent evaluations. Dissemination is given special emphasis on the grounds that in the past too little attention has been paid to dissemination in the setting of contracts and this has possibly exacerbated the non-utilization of evaluation findings.

Negotiating Conditions for Independent Evaluations

In another chapter in this volume Lawrence Stenhouse argues the case against independent evaluation of curriculum projects. Since I am concerned to promote and secure independent evaluation I should make it clear at the outset that both cases, his and mine, are embedded in different contexts of experience, and are responses to different problem structures. My recent evaluation experience, in common with a growing number of U.K. evaluators, illustrates the growth of studies of curriculum change that focus more than used to be the case on policy and executive levels of curriculum management, where the power and skills of the subjects of evaluation can be marshalled to pressurize evaluators in ways that interfere with their obligation to produce and make available public accounts of public programmes.

What seems to be necessary in such a context is to articulate, more precisely perhaps than we have in the past, the conditions necessary for independent inquiry. The notion of independence itself is a complex one as various authors have pointed out (MacDonald, 1976; Adelman, 1980). Independent of whom - the sponsor, the participants, the programme? Independent of what - bias, distortion, co-option? Independent for what purposes - scientific purity, dissemination, usability? And so on. We could easily add to the complexities.

For the purposes of this paper, however, I take independence to mean two things. First, it means that the evaluator should be free in the conduct of the evaluation to report events and different value perspectives fairly, accurately and impartially. It does not mean, as is often assumed, that the evaluator should simply offer a different or outside view from that provided by programme participants. Neither does it mean that the evaluator is working alone i.e. not for anyone. The position is more complex than that in the context of funding evaluations. Most evaluations are funded by one agency or another, whether it be a government agency like the SSRC or DES in the U.K. for example, charitable foundations like Nuffield or Gulbenkian in the U.K. and Ford Foundation in the U.S.A. or quasi-governmental agencies like the Schools Council in the U.K. In all three funding situations it is possible to operate on the principles of independence outlined here in conducting an evaluation. The fact that the evaluation is funded by a specific group does not mean that the evaluation is bought by that group, that the evaluator's obligation is only to that group, that the evaluator is seen as working for that group in the sense of providing them only with information that conforms to their values.

Secondly, independence means that the evaluator should be free to make results of the evaluation accessible to all groups who have a right to knowledge about the programme (though precisely who these groups are in any one context may need to be negotiated), that he has, if you like, an 'obligation to democratize his knowledge'. In publicly funded programmes of important educational issues this obligation to disseminate may be quite extensive.

For all practical purposes, in summary, independence means being able to conduct an evaluation 'without fear or favour', not subscribing to any one vested interest or allowing oneself to be predisposed to the view of any one group. This is not far short, in fact, of the Oxford Dictionary definition of independent:

> 'not depending upon the authority of another; not in a position of subordination, not subject to external control or rule; self-governing, free . . . not influenced or biased by the opinions of others . . . '

I start from a sense of apprehensiveness about contemporary trends that I see as threatening to independent evaluation. These trends are most marked and developed in the U.S.A. where the process of negotiating funding and site access has become extremely entangled, but are more noticeable in the U.K. when it comes to dissemination of findings.

Contract setting in the U.S.A. has been a dominant feature of sponsored evaluation for quite some time. Proposals for funds are subjected to detailed scrutiny in terms of aims, methodology, outcomes and costs and may be quite changed as a result: setting up conditions for fieldwork often involves mandatory negotiations with stakeholding groups including parents, teachers and administrators who are also able to exact changes. Contracts are usually written and agreements signed by the appropriate parties acknowledging acceptance of the study under the terms eventually agreed. The Right to Privacy Act (1974) added further protections for the subjects of research, compounding the growing complexity of pre-requisite clearance.

In England the equivalent requirements have for long been much less exacting. In the first place the pre-funding phase is usually confined to two parties, sponsor and evaluator or sponsor and director where curriculum projects are concerned. Arranging access is subsequent to the award of the contract, and typically informal. In the second place sponsors have been reluctant to specify their needs or convictions in any detail, leaving the evaluator largely free to follow his/her own preferences and restricting their role to a go/no-go decision. The contracts covering the evaluation usually take the form of a conventional research proposal sheet and an exchange of letters signifying support for the proposal from the sponsors and commitment to its implementation by the evaluator. In some cases, as in my recent experience (Simons, 1981) the contract can be much more informal than this and more distant. Sometimes the evaluator is only employed once the funding negotiations between the sponsor and director or institution are complete. In such circumstances opportunities for the evaluator to negotiate conditions for independence may be severely restricted.

But we should note some recent departures from this tradition that may indicate an emerging trend taking us closer to American practice. For instance, in the recently concluded five-year National Development Programme in Computer Assisted Learning, which funded more than thirty development and evaluation projects, the negotiation of contracts involved detailed discussions between programme and project directors concerning the aims, methods and costs of the proposals, and strict forms of subsequent accountability (see MacDonald and Jenkins, 1980). In a similar vein those now seeking access to the schools of the I.L.E.A. are faced with a daunting set of stringent requirements in the form of a contract drawn up by the administration and designed to secure administrative control of the investigative product.

Developments such as these are an early warning and the message is clear. If researchers and evaluators do not quickly seize the initiative in themselves articulating the kinds of agreements and contracts that are needed, the initiative will be taken by those perhaps less sensitive to and less informed about the conditions of worthwhile inquiry. It is to this purpose that this paper is addressed. It offers an identification of the issues at stake, and some suggestions designed to clarify and assert the case of independent inquiry.

That there is a need for greater articulation of the conditions for independent inquiry is evidenced also by the difficulties evaluators have encountered in conducting and disseminating evaluations. Let me cite a few examples here.

In the course of conducting an evaluation that looked as though its independence might be challendged by managerial controls I came across an evaluator who had negotiated in a contract what he thought were appropriate working conditions and relevant issues for an independent evaluation, only to find half-way through the evaluation that another contract existed (formulated between the sponsors and the institutions who held the grant before the evaluator was appointed) with different expectations of what was required from the evaluation. The evaluator asked to see this contract. He was not given access to it.

About the same time I came across another evaluator whose aspiration was to conduct an independent evaluation of a curriculum programme. She commented that she was finding it increasingly impossible to do so and was likely not to be able to report on the evaluation indepedently as the Director of the programme wanted and assumed that the evaluation would be integrated into his and the programme's total Report. Despite the evaluator's assertion of the independence of the evaluation the working assumption was that any findings of the evaluation would be subsumed in a total programme report.

A third example turns on the issue of censorship once an evaluation report had been written. In this particular case the evaluator wrote a report aspiring to tell the 'truth' of the progress of the innovation as he and his team saw it but this was objected to by a government department not on the grounds of the facts and events reported but the fear of the consequences on the community if certain facts were reported. The government department advised the evaluator to omit parts of the report. The issue here is a complex one and cannot simply be read, as one might first assume, as interference in the process of independent reporting. It is more a question of judiciousness in public reporting in certain circumstances (and who decides that) and also whether or not it is possible to arrive at a resolution that does not compromise the independence of the evaluation.

There is a fourth example I could cite from my own experience. This is documented fully in a separate paper (Simons, 1981), but I can cite one or two of the issues here. Unlike the first two examples, but not the third, most of the issues did not arise until an evaluation report had been written and negotiated with the personnel in the immediate programme who agreed that it was a fair, accurate and relevant account. It was at the managerial level that a dispute arose and this was over dissemination of the evaluation report to groups beyond the immediate programme. In summary, the issues at stake were these: conflicts of allegiance; confidentiality; service.

One of the major difficulties stemmed from the fact that the evaluator was working as an independent consultant for an academic institution under whose auspices the evaluation was being conducted, the evaluation itself having been commissioned by a local education authority. Like the evaluator in example one therefore I had to negotiate with two groups which had a named stake in the evaluation (quite separate from the negotiations pursued in the conduct of the evaluation with those involved in the implementation of the programme) although in this case there were no formal contracts. Expectations of the two groups varied widely, were sometimes in conflict, sometimes shifting. It was necessary for the academic institution to support the independent consultant who was conducting an independent evaluation on their behalf and they had expressly underwritten the independence of the evaluation at the outset by insisting that copyright of the evaluation reports lay with the institution. At the same time it was necessary for the institution to remain on good terms with the local education authority which seconded students to the institution's courses. The notion of independence came under severe scrutiny when the local education authority wanted to restrict ciruclation of an evaluation report of a publicly funded education programme that was conducted on independent principles and acknowledged by all concerned to be a fair, accurate and relevant account. The consequences for the community were not the issue here as in example three, rather more the invisible unspoken consequences for the local education authority.

One of the grounds on which the L.E.A. was disputing dissemination of the report was that they had given 'their' teachers a guarantee of blanket confidentiality that reports on their participation in this pilot experiment would not go beyond the L.E.A. except for reporting to the primary funding group, the E.E.C. This was not pointed out to me in the interview settling the agreement. Indeed had it been I would not have undertaken the evaluation. There is no way that an evaluator can publicly report on a programme that had guaranteed its participants blanket confidentiality. In conducting the evaluation I had adopted rigorous procedures for gaining access to, and release of, data, (for example, not reporting issues or comments on issues which people wished to keep private, asking permission for access to data, making it clear to participants that if verbatim comments were included in the report their permission would be sought, negotiating with participants at every stage). It was also clear, furthermore, from meetings in which all participants were involved, that the evaluation I was conducting was external and independent. This was emphasized by the managers in programme meetings time and time again, separating the independent external evaluation from the internal evaluation which was different and carried out by the project team and L.E.A. In short, there were two different uses of confidentiality in operation, the second of which only became known to me at the dispute stage, and these were in conflict. One protected the individual's right to keep information which was private to them, private; the other, the institution's discretion to choose what issues they would or would not make public.

Thirdly, there was disagreement about the function of the evaluation. In one of the minuted meetings early on in the dispute, the L.E.A. noted that one of the issues was whether the evaluator was or was not a 'tool of the Authority' carrying out a service for them. Clearly I thought that I was not, as I was conducting an independent external evaluation. Equally clearly the L.E.A. thought I was - conducting a service entirely for them. This difference of perspective was not apparent at the outset and became more entrenched as the dispute failed to be resolved.

These and other differences that became evident were between the L.E.A. and the evaluator concerning private promises the L.E.A. made to their employees and the procedures the evaluator had adopted to conduct an independent, external evaluation. At one point in the dispute the L.E.A. chose to involve the academic institution, claiming that their contract lay with the institution not the evaluator, and also claiming that they 'had reason to believe' that the institution would agree with them that the evaluation Report should not receive wider circulation. The evaluator thought (given that the institution had emphasized the independence of the evaluation in the initial agreement) that the institution would support the evaluation. The issue is slightly different here from that in example one. It was not that two definite contracts existed but rather that two eminent groups could choose to shift allegiances according to the emerging circumstances of the case.

Though these examples highlight the conflicts that arise when an independent evaluator finds the independence of the evaluation at risk, what they serve to illustrate is more the uncertainty that surrounds the practice of evaluation when different interests are in conflict. This uncertainty is further reflected in the refuge some have sought in legal advice to see if this will help clarify, resolve or defend conflicts that have arisen over evaluation practice and reporting. The seeking of legal advice has not been restricted to evaluators or indeed arisen from them. Managers, participants, sponsors have all raised issues which demand clarification and which point to the need for clearer articulation of appropriate working conditions for independent evaluations. Whether or not 'going legal' is the best way to resolve such issues is a point I will deal with later. In recognition of these difficulties our working group on ethics in evaluation devoted a session to legal issues. Two practising evaluators, including the author, contributed the following list of questions reflecting the growing uncertainties and concerns.

Questions for Seminar on Legal Aspects of Evaluation

Sometimes those who commission and pay for evaluations want to keep the results to themselves, and insist that the evaluation 'belongs' to them. Evaluators increasingly seek to publish their results and claim independence of their sponsors. Should a dispute over such an issue go to court, how might the following variables affect the outcome:

a) Initially the sponsors say that the evaluator would be free to publish, but subsequently changed their minds;
b) Initially the evaluator promises a confidential report but subsequently changes his mind;
c) The issue is never raised until the disagreement arises, and the contract makes no mention of it.

Evaluators often write reports which contain judgments of performance (of teachers, head, project directors etc.). These judgments can have serious consequences for the judged. We tend to call these judgements 'critiques'. What would make them 'libels'? If it could be proved that the libel had been endorsed as a 'fair comment' at any stage by the person concerned, would that invalidate a libel action?
Evaluators frequently use the device of confidentiality to reassure informants that what they say will not be used (i.e. made available to others) without their explicit authorization. Would the informant have any legal redress if the evaluator broke his promise?
Evaluators usually study pupils in schools, and write reports based on their observations, without the permission of the pupils or their parents. Is this legal? Do children or their parents have any rights with respect to such studies?
Is there a legal right to privacy, what does it say, and how might it apply to evaluation?
Would the act of anonomyzing an account protect the evaluator against prosecution?
Can the possession of copyright be used to deny access to an evaluation report, or does the establishment of copyright require the lodging of the report in specified libraries, thus guaranteeing public access?
How important in law are the terms of the contract between the sponsors and the evaluators, and what is the difference between an agreement and a contract?

Managers, sponsors, participants may well draw up a different list of questions from their respective standpoints or interests although I suspect that many of the persistently troubling issues of confidentiality, contract status, privacy and publication would appear in any list.

These legal issues are addressed directly in "Guidelines II", in this volume. Here it is sufficient to note that the fact, that we are now thinking about such issues, is a clear reflection of the experience of conflict between evaluators, sponsors of evaluations, and subjects of evaluations.

At the same time we should also note that in some recent policy evaluation studies, evaluators have simply avoided the issues by contractural capitulation. For instance, in the E.E.C.'s first major venture in so-called independent evaluations of pilot educational experiments in the Transition from School to Work programme, all but one of its twenty-eight contracted evaluations are subject to total bureaucratic control. It seems from this that the rise of the E.E.C. as a major sponsor of evaluation is likely to intensify managerial control of the evaluation community.

One way of avoiding some of these difficulties is for the evaluator, sponsor and participating groups to formulate mutually agreed positions on essential issues into a written contract. Some of the issues that need to be taken into account in setting such contracts have been well documented by Stake (1976). In an assignment for the Centre for Educational Research and Innovation (O.E.C.D.), he sought and presented the responses of a number of administrators to the following five major issues:

- the degree of specificity of evaluation plans;
- the specificity of design and length of time necessary for negotiating contracts;
- the relative importance of and constraints on agreements on access and publication;
- the practice of evaluators meeting the needs of the research community, not the sponsor;
- guidelines for the use of a prestige panel to investigate programmes.

He also presented the views of a number of researchers on the following issues:

- the freedom of the evaluator to choose the methods of inquiry;
- the degree to which the evaluator should link into basic research questions;
- whether there should be any restriction on the evaluator publishing results in professional journals;
- whether the evaluator should ask for assurances that:

  i) he can follow his own conscience in reporting malpractices;
  ii) his findings will be given attention,

iii)   his findings will not be used to support claims they do not.

Published in the same account is a checklist of questions to raise in negotiating a contract between the evaluator and sponsor (Stake, 1976).

From a slightly different standpoint the influential writings of Ernest House throughout the past decade have had a considerable impact in raising the consciousness of American evaluators regarding the conditions of fair and impartial evaluation. (See House, 1980.)

In this country too, there is increasing consensus among practising evaluators about the need for an initial contract. MacDonald (1978), Parlett (1977) and Adelman, Kemmis and Jenkins, (1975), have argued for several years now that a written contract should be established between the evaluator and the sponsor to secure procedures for conducting the study, to prevent misunderstanding and to provide a basis for review in cases of dispute.

Rather less has been written however about problems of independence which confront evaluators in working through evaluations, for a major exception see Adelman (1980), and it is these problems I wish to address.

In one sense the problems are made more acute by the British tradition of informal understandings. It sometimes seems curious to American colleagues that in the U.K. we have to negotiate for independence of dissemination, if not the right to report, on publicly funded programmes. Initial negotiations may be more stringent in the U.S.A. but access to the completed report more open. The differences are very much context bound and reflect, as many have commented before, the tendency of the English system to operate informally, often secretly; and the American system to be procedurally and constitutionally more open. (See, for instance, Kogan, 1979, House, 1976, Smith, 1980.)

The crux of my argument is this. Firstly, as I have already stated, there is a growing trend in this country for evaluations to be subject to restrictive contractual controls. Secondly, the tradition of informality, although it seems on the face of it to promote freedom of operation on the part of the evaluator, actually results in much greater evaluator vulnerability to controlling pressures from those who have power in the system. In other words, in the event of the evaluation developing in ways that were not anticipated and are not desired by powerful sponsors or subjects, the evaluator seldom has the protection of a written agreement that specifies the meaning and consequences of independent evaluation. The problem is compounded by the fact that many evaluators have relatively low status, work in isolation and are at risk in a career sense compared with those in powerful institutional positions who employ or sponsor their work.

The answer lies, I would suggest, in two propositions. The first is that the evaluator ensure that he or she has sufficient institutional backing that can be called upon in the event of the independence of the evaluation being put at risk. The second proposition is that the evaluator at the outset engages all those concerned in a dialogue about foreshadowed issues leading to a clear written agreement about the conduct, outcomes and dissemination of the study, although quite how tightly such agreements should be written is debatable. Of course, I am aware, as others have pointed out (Adelman, 1980; Parlett, 1976; Stake, 1976), that early negotiations need to be revisited throughout the study to examine their appropriateness in the light of developing or changing relationships and knowledge. Such a review of the initial agreement should be built into the contract or provision made for any one of the parties to the evaluation to suggest a review.

Quite how useful such contracts have been in resolving disputes is little documented. In the face of difficulties in the field, some evaluators, sponsors and participants have sought legal advice and leaned strongly towards the legal framework as one possible way of resolving disputes.

While the legal dimensions of the process and practice of evaluation and social science in general has not been given much attention and perhaps ought to be considered more (see, for example, Smith, 1975), I would like to suggest here a note of caution. It is by no means the case that invoking legal procedures to settle a dispute or tighten a contract in evaluation is going to produce better conditions for evaluation. In the first place the kinds of problems which face evaluators may not be of the same order as those which led to the creation of the laws. In the second place, too formalized or legalized a contract may be dysfunctional to the whole process of evaluation where the aspiration is to create a climate of trust. One set of assumptions (legal) for settling disputes may conflict with the evaluator's assumptions about the nature of the social process of conducting research and evaluation. The legality of contract setting, moreover, is only one aspect of a whole process of evaluation including the conduct of the study and the reporting of findings and should not be seen to dominate.

It is far better for the whole process of evaluation in my view to concentrate on clarifying the issues through dialogue than through recourse to the law. The process takes time but each resolution through negotiation contributes to the educative process as well as the resolution of the particular conflict. I am not sure at this point if recourse to the law, even in cases of dispute, will do anything but delay the process of gradually making more information accessible and open to public discussion through evaluation studies.

In the interests of trying to promote more effective negotiation and appropraite conditions for independent inquiry I have formulated some rules of thumb, derived from experience of evaluations, which have helped me begin to think about the most useful working conditions for an independent evaluation.

Rules of Thumb and Caveats

Sponsors in the initial contract stage are more concerned with sorting out details of finance than with the principles and procedures by which an evaluation is to be conducted. The onus is on the evaluator, time and protocol allowing, to persuade them to listen. Sponsors' prime concern at the initial stage of negotiation is with ensuring that the methodological stance of the evaluation suits their purposes or is academically respectable and the researcher is a credible person for the task.

Evaluations are rarely set up concurrent with a project; in the subsequent pressure to provide evaluation, negotiations are often rushed and in the process critical issues are not addressed by either the evaluator or the sponsor. The contract for the evaluation needs to be open enough to allow the evaluator to negotiate conditions for conducting the evaluation once he/she has had time to assess what is needed. The time factor may conflict with the sponsor's and the evaluator's necessity to sign and seal the agreement.

If the sponsors and the participants in the initial negotiations and throughout the evaluation are not asking questions which could later become problematic the onus is on the evaluator to raise them.

The extent to which different agreements may need to be made with different groups involved in the evaluation cannot always be ascertained at the outset. Initial agreements should therefore not be binding until the needs of each group are clearly defined. The evaluator should not accept decisions which sponsors make on behalf of participants but should insist on the right to negotiate with all groups which constitute potential data for the evaluation. The sponsor is likely to assume that the negotiation lies solely between the evaluator and the sponsor. But there are other groups with which agreements have to be made. The evaluator has to ensure that the agreements made with each group are clearly understood and respected by the other groups involved. Those who sponsor evaluation do not own it or have more control over the product than is compatible with the agreements made with other stakeholders.

The onus is on the evaluator to establish who within the organization/s has the authority to negotiate and to take decisons. Sometimes these are not the same people. The problem is that it is often difficult to get this information, especially in advance; and authority may shift as difficulties arise.

The person within the sponsoring organization gaining agreement for the study should make the policy roles of all the people likely to be involved in the evaluation explicit.

Those responsible for employing the evaluation must make available to him/her all relevant agreements, made with stakeholders, that may have implications for the conduct or boundaries of the evaluation. (Adelman, 1980.)

The agreements reached as a result of negotiations on these and other issues such as the ones raised by House and Stake should be embodied in a contract which is made available to all those who are parties to the evaluation study. Such contracts should go a long way towards anticipating, avoiding or helping resolve some of the conflicts which have characterized and undermined recent evaluation studies. They will not in themselves, however, necessarily resolve the particular issues in a case. These must be negotiated and discussed and an agreeement reached through continuous dialogue with the different parties to the evaluation. Contracts can never replace trust (and one could argue in certain cases, depending upon how they are interpreted and used, that they could serve to undermine trust) and an acceptable and reasonable way of working together. The purpose of contracts should be to clarify the function of evaluation, and the procedures by which the evaluation is to be conducted and reported. They could also help to make clear to all those concerned the extent to which any particular study can be considered independent.

References

Adelman, C. (1980) 'Some Dilemmas of Institutional Evaluation and their Relationship to Preconditions and Procedures'. Studies in Educational Evaluation Vol. 6, pp. 165-183.

Adelman, C., Kemmis, S. and Jenkins, D. (1976) 'Rethinking Case Study: notes from the second Cambridge Conference', Cambridge Journal of Education, Vol. 6, no. 3, Michaelmas Term.

House, E.R. (1978) 'Justice in Evaluation', in Glass, G.V. (ed) Evaluation Studies -Review Annual, Vol. 1, Beverley Hills, California: Sage Publications.

House, E.R. (1980) Evaluating with Validity, Sage Publications.

Kogan, M. (1979) The Politics of Educational Change, Fontana.

MacDonald, B. and Jenkins, D. (1980) UNCAL: The Final Report of the Independent Educational Evaluation of the National Development Programme in Computer Assisted Learning, Centre for Applied Research in Education, University of East Anglia.

Parlett, M. (1976) 'Training for Case Study Research and Evaluation', in Simons, H. (ed) (1980) Towards a Science of the Singular: essays about case study in educational research and evaluation, Occasional Publication 10, Centre for Applied Research in Education, University of East Anglia.

Parlett, M. and Dearden, G. (1981) Introduction to Illuminative Evaluation: Studies in Higher Education, Society for Research into Higher Education, Guildford. First issued 1977 by Pacific Soundings Press.

MacDonald, B. (1978) 'Letters from a Headmaster', in Simons, H. (ed) (1980) Towards a Science of the Singular: essays about case study in educational research and evaluation, Occasional Publication 10, Centre for Applied Research in Education, University of East Anglia.

Simons, H. (1981) 'Case Studying Superordinates: the power politics of policy evaluation'. Paper presented for a symposium on Case Study in Policy Evaluation: Paradoxes of Popularity, American Educational Research Association's Annual Meeting, Los Angeles.

Smith, L.M. (1975) 'Some Not So Random Thoughts on Doing Fieldwork: the interplay of values', in Simons, H. (ed) (1980) Towards a Science of the Singular: essays about case study in educational research and evaluation, Occasional Publication 10, Centre for Applied Research in Education, University of East Anglia.

Smith, L.M. (1980) 'Reflecting on Cambridge III'. Notes arising from discussion at the Cambridge III Conference on Naturalistic

Inquiry in Educational Research and Evaluation, Wolfson Court, Girton College, Cambridge, December 1979. Washington University, mimeo.

Stake, R.E. (1976) Evaluation Programmes: the need and the response, a collection of resource materials prepared by R.E. Stake for the Centre for Educational Research and Innovation (CERI) and Organization for Economic Co-operation and Development (OECD) Paris.

Chapter 6

EVALUATION: A CASE OF RESEARCH IN CHAINS?

Ian Jamieson

Introduction

The papers in this volume refer to a wide variety of evaluations that have been conducted in the field of education. The authors concentrate on the distinctive ethical questions that are presumed to arise in those research enterprises that they have dubbed 'evaluation'. A review of these papers forces this author to ask what is distinctive about those studies which have been labelled as evaluations, or evaulation research, composed with a research exercise which is thought not to constitute evaluation. This paper will stress the importance of establishing evaluation research as a distinct research activity, and will show that many of the major problems with which evaluators feel they are faced, particularly the ethical ones, follow from a failure to recognise that evaluation research is not the same as academic research.

The nature of evaluation

Many of the papers in this volume reveal the extremely diverse nature of work that goes on under the name of evaluation. Evaluations conducted in the illuminative tradition, include the use of participant observation, historiography, film documentary, legal advocacy, investigative journalism, literary criticism, bidding strategy in card games, client-centred therapy, cultural critique, the scrutiny of legal documents, ordinary conversation, and policy analysis. (1) What is it that holds all these activities together and pronounces the evaluations? It is tempting to follow Dennis Wrong's (1964) answer to the question, 'What is Sociology' by replying that evaluation is what evaulators do. This inductive answer does beg an important question however: what does the claim 'to be an evaluator' entail? It surely makes no sense to allow anybody to claim the status of evaluator, or to grace their activity with the label evaluation. This is no mere linguistic quibble, because unless the term evaluation does refer to a distinctive set of activities, then it is hardly possible to discuss the ethical or methodological problems involved in evaluation.

The claim to be an evaluator is surely different in kind from the claim (say) to be a psychologist or an historian. In the latter case the claim is to a body of knowledge allied to certain principles of method. Although it is true that there may be energetic disputes about what that knowledge is, and what constitutes the methodological principles, it's important that certain sorts of activities are deemed not to qualify. To be an evaluator entails being employed by a sponsor to carry out a specific form of research. The research tends to concentrate on a delimited programme of action, e.g. a project or experiment and is largely focussed on the factors which are considered to be important for programme success and are within the control of programme operators. If evaluation is considered to be a special form of sponsored research then it is possible to understand a key feature of many of the papers in this volume. Many of the contributors focus on the constraints that are placed on the evaluator as researcher, the implication being that academic research is much less constrained. The implication is that the sponsor tends to be the major source of constraint in framing, conducting and publishing the research. The argument would run that it is a common practice for the sponsor to define the problem to be researched; would exercise the right to be consulted over the methods of enquiry, would generally specify the audience to be addressed in reporting and may even control public access to the results. The sponsoring organisation can claim these 'rights' by virtue of the fact that it has paid for the evaluation and it is technically its property. In the case of a non-sponsored evaluation, the evaluator restricts himself by carrying out the research in such a way that the results would be likely to prove acceptable to policy makers and potential sponsors.

Research and Evaluation Constraints

I know that there are many evaluators on both sides of the Atlantic who feel constrained by the sorts of restrictions which I have briefly referred to above. Furthermore, those constraints are made to feel more onerous by virtue of the evaluators own academic training and experience, and by their involvement in a set of cultural values which place a high premium on what is usually called academic freedom. Thus many evaluators have had successful experience as independent researchers (perhaps on a Ph.D. programme) where the research problem and the theoretical orientation and methodology were freely chosen and there was not hindrance to publication. As researchers these individuals became part of the scientific community and were expected to pursue the 'truth' in an unfettered way. Whilst it would be difficult to deny the existence of these widely held frustrations amongst evaluators as psychological phenomena, the logic of their case seems rather less convincing. In the first place the statement of constraints that flow from the research being contract or sponsored research, must be a tendency statement only. It is just not true that sponsors always define the research problem tightly, or that they invariably demand to be consulted over issues of methodology or theory, or that they attempt to place restrictions on the publication of results. Indeed, in the case of one of the largest contractors of educational evaluation in England and Wales, the Schools Council, such constraints have invariably not been applied, at least formally.

On the other side of the coin one certainly needs to examine the view that 'academic research' is lacking in constraints. Thus against the view that the academic is free to determine how the problem should be framed and subsequently tackled in terms of theory and method as well as being free to publish his results, we must set the following constraints. Social research invariably costs money and the amount of money available often sets stringent parameters to the way in which problems that would remain inaccessible but for the funding. Another major problem for 'independent' social researchers is that of access - in the case of evaluations in education, to pupils/students, teachers, administrators and institutions. Of course all evaluators don't necessarily have free access to everything that they would like, and because they are invariably evaluating special programmes or projects they are more likely to encounter problems like the 'Hawthorne effect', even so the problem of access tends to be greatly amerliorated for evaluators.

Not only are evaluators arguably less constrained in terms of funding and access than similarly placed independent researchers, but it is possible to argue that some of the freedoms of the academic researcher are more illusory than real. Let us take the issue of freedom to publish one's results. The demand of some evaluators that the sponsor should publish the results 'untouched' does not really have a parallel in the academic world. In the case of journals the academic researcher has to convince his peers in the scientific community that his results are both significant and sound, and adjustments are often called for. As Kuhn (1970) has argued, the scientific community can be as resistant to divergent views which transgress the paradigm of what constitutes 'normal science' as any sponsor of an evaluation. Turning to the question of commercial publication, clearly the publisher has to weigh a number of considerations alongside whether the findings of the research are 'true' or not. Arguably, commercial considerations are at least as important as the soundness of the findings for the majority of the publishers.

The publication of results becomes such a sensitive issue for evaluators because it is thought to involve a set of fundamental moral issues concerned with censorship and the suppression of the truth. Yet the ethical issue is not nearly so clear cut as this. In the first place is it 'the truth' that is at issue? In the social sciences at least the relativity of knowledge, or the substitution of knowledge for understanding, is a widely held position. The rise of the illuminative school in educational evaluation bears witness to similar doubts about the epistemological claims of the positivist position in education. Framed this way it becomes the question of the publication of whose truth? The merits of the illuminative mode of analysis, which invariably attempts to provide a variety of views of the same phenomena, are then clear.

It can be persuasively argued that the publication of results is a fundamental goal in scientific research of any description, but is the same true of evaluation research? I would argue that because many people engaged as evaluators fail to appreciate the difference between conducting an evaluation as against a piece of what I have called academic research that many of the problems surrounding the publication issue arise. Whereas evaluators may publish their results it should not be assumed that this is a normal activity in the same way that the publication of scientific results is. Many evaluations are conceived by the sponsor as providing a service to itself as the funding body e.g. 'Tell us how that programme of social action we have sponsored is working', or as a service to a particular group of practitioners. In the latter case the evaluation is often, and perhaps most usefully, formative, and the question of publication does not arise anyway.

I have argued that a key feature of evaluation research is that it is sponsored research, an evaluator is engaged to research a prescribed issue, problem or programme. I have further maintained that whereas a fundamental goal of academic research is the publication of results to the scientific community this is not the case for evaluation. I have argued this second point on the grounds that evaluators are primarily paid to provide a service to the funding body. This has implications for the sorts of questions to which evaluators address themselves, the methods they use to answer those questions, and the form of the reporting. Primarily, evaluators address themselves to the questions that the sponsor requires answering. One might contrast this with the world of academic research where the questions are framed by the individual researcher working in the context of the academic community of his peers. Of course there will be evaluators who claim that the sponsor did not influence the framing of the questions or the form of reporting. I think that most of these cases can be accounted for in one of two ways. The selection of evaluators very often takes care of a great many potential problems. Potential evaluators who are not sympathetic to the interests and views of the sponsor, or who do not possess what is considered to be an 'appropriate' academic/research background are usually not employed. Thus potential problems are overcome by what Jenkins and North (1980) would call 'matching'. The same occurs in journalism and partly accounts for the fact that few journalists complain of censorship. Influence can also be brought to bear on evaluators in more subtle ways. Most evaluators are engaged on short term contracts so that if they wish to remain in the evaluation business they have to constantly re-enter the market place. Thus there are sound economic reasons why evaluators should conform to the wishes of the sponsor. The sponsor may not need to exercise any overt pressure at all; it's a classic case of non-decision making.

Reporting Evaluation and Research Findings

Not only are the questions to which the evaluator addresses himself often not entirely under his control but often neither is the form of the report (assuming that a report is called for; I have already suggested that many evaluations are designed only as formative exercises and no summative report is sought). My argument would be that in practice such a choice of ways in which to report would be largely illusory, as the needs and interests of the sponsor largely determine the form of the report, in much the same way as the norms of what constitutes an acceptable journal article in psychology determine the form of such academic 'reports'. Not only is it a fact that different sponsors require different reports from different evaluations, but the authors don't seem to distinguish between academic research and evaluation. Thus it is difficult to see how Richardson's (1973) study of Nailsea School or Lacey's (1970) study of Hightown Grammar could qualify as evaluations, as neither represent examples of sponsored research.

Evaluation reports and research reports not only have different audiences but their main objectives are different. The goal of the research report is the enhancement of understanding and knowledge via publication to the scientific community. The main goal of the evaluation report is to inform and/or influence decision makers, (and whether they are successful in this endeavour is not a relevant consideration, although consistent lack of success may encourage evaluators to embrace other goals coterminously). Of course, all this is both too simple and too clear cut. Clearly many research reports eventually influence decision makers. Lacey's work on Hightown Grammar certainly influenced the debate on selection. On the other hand more than a few evaluation reports have contributed to an explanation of phenomena. Yet despite the obvious truth of these observations the relative emphasis of the two activities must be different.

There are two major reasons why research reports tend to differ from evaluation reports: the first relates to the object of the enquiry; the second to the demands and interests of the sponsors. The focus of evaluations is most typically on attempts at social engineering, largely of the variety which Popper (1972) would designate as 'piecemeal'. In other words evaluators look at programmes of social action -'projects' or 'experiments', - which are trying to tackle a problem which has been identified by a social agency (usually the sponsor) as worthy of attention. The nature of the subject matter does not of itself distinguish evaluation from research, although it is the case that whereas the great majority of evaluations, certainly in education are focussed on specific programmes of social action, published research reports are very much more catholic in their interests. The distinguishing feature of the evaluation report lies more in the sorts of questions which it addresses, and they way it tackles them. The sponsor is typically interested in essentially practical details, i.e. a stress on the sorts of variables and factors which are capable of change or manipulation. His interest is in a report which allows him to assess the worth of a programme or project, to identify its strengths and weaknesses. Thus sponsors tend not to be overly concerned with factors or variables, which, although they might have considerable explanatory power, are not really capable of manipulation. The academic researcher, on the other hand, has his focus of attention set not by an outside sponsor, nor by the demands of realpolitik. His problem is typically theoretically constituted, his focus is on variables which tend to have explanatory power.

The difference of emphasis in the content of the evaluation as against the research report can be related back to our remarks on the publication results.   One of the reasons why the primary goal of evaluation is not the publication of results is simply that the focus of interest tends to be both too particular (a particular project or experiment), and within the particular case too much centred on factors which are of interest for reasons connected more to the possibilities of social action than to explanatory power.   Of course, evaluations (or what purport to be evaluations) do get published in academic journals, and they typically attract just the sort of criticism that we would expect from this analysis – that they focus on a narrow range of manipulable variables at the expense of wider issues, that they are either atheoretical or their theoretical underpinning is not made explicit.   It might be argued that not all published accounts deriving from evaluation work are open to such criticisms and this point must be conceded.   In England at least this is partly accounted for by the lack of a career structure for people engaged in evaluation work.   There is consultant movement between the ranks of those engaged in academic work and those involved in evaluation activities. The effect of this lack of job security on the part of evaluators is that many of them operate 'two agendas' when they carry out an evaluation.   The first agenda relates to satisfying the requirements of the sponsor, and here data relating to particular <u>practical</u> concerns of the sponsoring agency are dutifully collected.   The second agenda relates to a set of wider more theoretically grounded concerns.   This data can constitute a valuable resource for an evaluator who may soon have to move back into the academic market and who wishes to bring rather more than mere evaluation experience with him.   The result can be the publication of another view of the project or experiment.   It is not an evaluation report, the frame has changed and it now constitutes a research report.

Reactions to Evaluation Constraints

It has been argued that because the focus of evaluation research tends to be on specific activities, e.g. a project or an experiment, and that the sponsor is invariably interested in the evaluator's assessment of the activity in terms of success or failure, then this raises some critical dilemmas that are rarely present, at least in such an acute form, in academic research.   In the most difficult case, the sponsor of the evaluation is also the employer of the personnel working on the project that is being evaluated.   In addition the sponsor is specifically interested in whether the project is achieving its stated aims.   In such a situation there are clearly many claims that can be laid at the door of the evaluator of which the obligation to tell 'the truth' is merely one, and perhaps not one that many of the interest groups involved would support to the exclusion of all other claims.   Many evaluators see themselves as becoming increasingly powerless: the sponsor constrains their activities and frequently ignores their report in decision making; the rights of the subjects of the evaluation are increasingly recognised and protected; there is a lack of any career structure for evaluators and therefore a lack of incentive amongst some to perform well. Two reactions follow: in the first place more and more evaluators see the political advantage of a democratic evaluation style, i.e. one that stresses the essential relativity of truth, and aims to present the diversity of views in any particular situation. Whatever the philosophical merits of such a position it effectively removes the evaluator from the 'heat of the kitchen'. The second reaction sees evaluators courting the idea of professionalisation. Professionalisation is seen as an effective and legitimate way of exercising counterveiling power, of loosening some of the chains that bind. It is unlikely that such a move sould do anything to promote their cause. In the first place it is difficult to see how a professional organisation could counteract the power of the sponsoring bodies. Evaluators and their body of practice do not appear to possess any of the fundamental requirements of strong control over their own affairs. For example, using the criteria put forward by Johnson (1972) we find that the social origins of evaluators would not stand comparison to a powerful professional group like doctors or lawyers; the methods of evaluation are not distinctively different from those of social science research in general (most textbooks on evaluation methodology cover similar areas to those on social science) and this means that the potential supply of persons technically capably of undertaking an evaluation is relatively large. Finally, whereas most powerful professional groups derive some of their power from the fact that the consumers tend to consist of a relatively heterogeneous and fragmented mass - exactly the opposite is the case in evaluation. It seems likely that the only effect that the existence of a professional body of evaluation researchers would have, would be the production of an ethical code of practice for its own members, along the lines of the codes which exist for professional social scientists in both Britain and America. Ironically these would constitute yet one more constraint. I would argue that there is much merit in the present British situation where people move freely between academic research and evaluation research. A professional evaluator who depends for his livelihood on securing contracts from sponsors is more likely to 'adapt' his judgement than one who is likely to find his next job in an academic environment where the canons of objectivity and 'truth' are permanent.

Conclusion

Ethical discourse insofar as it is concerned with events in the real world is essentially concerned with the question of how people ought to behave. The question of moral behaviour can never be considered in purely abstract terms, it always has to be grounded in a certain context. The main argument of this paper has been that academic research and evaluation research provide essentially different contexts for research activity, and thus what is regarded as moral behaviour differs accordingly. I have further argued that the distinction between research and evaluation has a good deal of practical significance for evaluators. These individuals employed as evaluators who act and expect others to act as though they were academic researchers, are likely to experience a good deal of psychological stress. This is because they are operating with one set of codes of conduct, whilst others (notably the sponsor) is operating with a different set. The problems that this creates are likely to be seen by both parties as ethical problems, and they will characteristically revolve round issues like, truth, freedom to publish, responsiblity to various groups, etc.

The growing calls for the professionalisation of the community of evaluators has many sources: it reflects amongst other things the rapid growth of sponsored research in education and in particular the rise of the social or educational 'experiment' or 'programme' designed to solve or ameliorate a particular problem. It also represents a desire on the part of many evaluators to have some influence on the codes of conduct for evaluation research. At the extreme it is a demand that they should be treated as academic researchers, although such demands are always dressed up in the moral clothes of 'academic freeedom', the 'sanctity of the truth'. At worst this is no more than the exchange of one set of moral lawmakers for another, the exchange of a code of conduct laid down by the sponsor for one emanating from a professional association. What evidence we have of the operation of powerful professional groups suggests that the public interest may fare little better under 'professional care' than under the care of the organisations sponsoring research. This is not to argue of course, that the behaviour of evaluation sponsors should not be carefully scrutinised – the powerful have a greater responsibility in our society to uphold the principles of moral behaviour in the research setting than the weak. Such a duty should be remembered by sponsors when they employ evaluators and by evaluators when they research their subjects.

REFERENCES

Bachrach, P. and Baratz, M. (1962) 'Two Faces of Power' American Science Review 1956.

Jenkins, D. and North, R. (1980) Evaluation Reports: steady state in Big bang? mimeo. New University of Ulster.

Johnson, T. (1972) Professions and Power. MacMillan, London.

Kuhn, T. A. (1970) The Structure of Scientific Revolutions. University of Chicago Press, Chicago.

Lacey, C. (1970) Hightown Grammar: the School and a Social System. Manchester University Press, Manchester.

Popper, K. (1972) Conjectures and Refutations: The Growth of Scientific Knowledge. Routledge & Kegan Paul, London.

Richardson, E. (1973) The Teachers, The School and The Task of Management. Routledge & Kegan Paul, London.

Wrong, D. (1961) "The Oversocialised Conception of Man". American Sociological Review. XXVI pp 183-192.

Chapter 7

EVALUATING CURRICULUM EVALUATION

Lawrence Stenhouse

Introduction

Curriculum evaluation was conceived in a context of 'curriculum development' or 'curriculum reform' rather than one of 'curriculum research'. Evaluation was to be the traditional researchers' critical contribution to a movement driven, it was to be supposed, by the creative, but uncritical, enthusiasm of the curriculum reformer. In fact, curriculum evaluation as such did not attract a great deal of support in this country, as contrasted with the United States. Most curriculum projects were not evaluated; and, drawn partly by the accountability movement, evaluators have now turned their attention to the evaluation of policies and institutions.

In the curriculum field it is important to build on the research, rather than the development tradition of the curriculum movement of the 60s and 70s. The basic stance is to treat curricular action and process - whether existent or developing - as problematic and hypothetical, and to value it for the learning and development it will support in teachers and students. If teachers and teaching are not improving as a result of the curriculum, then research-led development is needed.

In short, curriculum is to be seen as an area of action research. This demands an integration of the research spirit into curriculum activity, a digestion of the evaluative tradition into curriculum research. In the curriculum field, evaluation as such has made a valuable contribution, but its independence is now dysfunctional. The research spirit should not be exiled into evaluation, but naturalized in curriculum research. By the extent that evaluation continues to be needed as a discrete specialist field in curriculum work we can gauge a failure of design or direction in curriculum research.

I define research as systematic inquiry made public. The traditional purpose of research is to build out understanding. The time honoured way of doing this is through the interpretation of evidence, and history is the archetypal example of this procedure. More recently science has tackled the problem of extending understanding by building theory. All research - even in art or music -is speculative or hypothetical; no answers are available unless we can conjure them from the mass of information around us by a principle of relevance which turns some information into evidence.

Educational research ought in my view to be essentially addressed to problems in the understanding of educational practice, and it is therefore of vital importance that it be addressed to educational practitioners. This point is not infrequently obscured by the fact that both psychologists and sociologists conduct research in education and handle it within their own disciplines. My own thinking about educational research is not dissimilar in perspective from that of Joseph Schwab, except that my roots are sufficiently in the humanistic tradition to prevent my having to rebel against the assumptions of positivist social science. These assumptions have never been mine.

My basic position in this chapter is that curriculum research is concerned with understanding the interplay of conceptions of knowledge, attempts to express them in the art of teaching and the social and physical contexts of those attempts. That is, for example what the Humanities Curriculum Project was about. And such curriculum research is central to educational research. Anything which encourages a developmental rather than a research view of curriculum is deleterious to the optimum improvement of educational practice. Evaluation, which uses more or less the same techniques as research, has as its purpose the making of judgements about the merits or demerits of policies, practices, institutions or persons. Curriculum evaluation tends to treat practice as if it were founded on choices or decisions rather than on understanding and the development of the art of teaching. Thereby it encourages a developmental view of curriculum, and suggests - wrongly in my view - that curriculum workers do not require research skills, which instead are supplied by the evaluator.

In particular, I question the idea of independent evaluation. Not only does the conception carry with it the notion that there is some wholly objective dispassionate research which profits from disengagement from practice - an idea I cannot accept - but also it awards the evaluator such power over and profit from the ideas of the curriculum researcher that no curriculum researcher is likely to take up that contract twice. The developer/evaluator distinction promotes a spearation of action and inquiry that seems to me to have disastrous implications for and effects upon the practice of education.

Let's look back and try to get a perspective on these issues.

In 1967, when I was appointed Director of the Humanities Curriculum Project, the main precedents in curriculum research and development in this country were the Nuffield Science projects. Insofar as these had an element of evaluation in them, it was concerned with the revision of teaching materials in the light of teacher judgement. Their research content was also narrow. At the invitation of the Nuffield Foundation I spent a morning with Hilda Misselbrook, the Director of the Nuffield Secondary Science Project to get a briefing on how to conduct my new trade. Hilda Misselbrook was a good way ahead of us. Her project was not at that time involved in evaluation other than the evaluation of materials through teacher feed-back, and to the best of my memory she was already resisting evaluation proposals. Indeed, though there was in the end an evaluation of Nuffield Secondary Science, it did not begin until 1969. The project ran from 1965 to 1970. The Primary French Project was being evaluated, but there appeared to be no strong desire for the evaluation of their projects either in the Nuffield Foundation or in the Schools Council.

Two years before our project started, in 1965, the Schools Council had set up a working party on curriculum evaluation. That working party adopted what is now commonly known as the objectives model, and as I understand it, its work did not arouse great enthusiasm among the Schools Council's committees. It was partly as a consequence of the Schools Council's failure to take up and push the working party's report that Stephen Wiseman and Douglas Pidgeon, both of whom were members of the working party, wrote their book on curriculum evaluation which was published in 1970. That was the year when the main phase of the Humanities Curriculum Project ended.

From 1968 onwards I had been arguing against the objectives model in curriculum research and development. It would be difficult now to believe the violence of the attacks made on me when I tried to make this view pulbic. In retrospect I believe that, though part of that violence was the frictional heat not infrequently generated in academic discussion, some of it can be explained in terms of the politics of research.

The educational research establishment saw in the 1960s unprecedented investment in educational research and development by Nuffield and the Schools Council. It wanted to get its hands on the resources being made available and it was in danger of being left out. Too much of its investment had been in the technology of testing, and it had neglected the kind of research into teaching and schooling covered by Gage's (1963) Handbook of Research on Teaching. Its newest development was in analytic philosophy, where worthwhile but limited contributions were being made. Meanwhile, the money that the research establishment coveted was being given to project directors who were outside that establishment.

The picture of the situation that the educational research establishment promoted in its bid for evaluation contracts can be illustrated by quotation from Wiseman and Pidgeon's book:

> "The curriculum reformer is always an enthusiast with a keen sense of urgency and a strong motivation to get on with the job and produce the goods. And so he dives head-long into the production of materials, since he himself knows (or believes he knows) where he wants to go . . . the enthusiast is convinced from the outset that his new curriculum is bound to be successful designed as it is to rectify the shortcomings of the old one."

Wiseman and Pidgeon concede that the description of the curriculum reformer is exaggerated. But I would be prepared to concede that there are some curriculum developers who fit this description.

In a section headed 'Developers v. Evaluators' Wiseman and Pidgeon observe that 'tension between developer and evaluator will never be completely eliminated, since they have essentially different stances and different roles'. Their view of these different stances and roles is clear.

> "It must be recognised that curriculum innovators are essentially creative; the evaluator's vocabulary is foreign to them, his philosophy but vaguely apprehended, his credo often distrusted."

And they note:

> "There is a tendency for the educational psychologist and the psychometrist to take a hard, sceptical, rigorous 'scientific' line."

Now, this typecasting was one which I, as a curriculum developer, was not prepared to accept. For ten years I had been teaching educational theory in a university and a college of education. My basic qualification was the Scottish M.Ed. which would qualify me as an evaluator in Wiseman and Pidgeon's terms. And worse still, I took the view that the psychometrists -including Wiseman and Pidgeon -had got their noses so far down into the techniques of mental measurement that they had almost lost touch with the nature of scientific - or non-scientific research. They were even prepared apparently to abandon the hypothetico-deductive structure of science, which one might associate with their 'hard, sceptical, rigorous "scientific" ' line, and test the objectives framed by developers out of enthusiasm rather than hypotheses generated by scientists out of observation! Unlike some of my colleagues in curriculum research, I believe that psychometric tests are useful in the field; but though I am prepared to concede that there are some skilled psychometrists who have broad grasp and scientific intelligence - Lee Cronbach and Gene Glass, for example - my impression is that 95% of psychometrists - and perhaps a rather higher percentage in this country -need to work within structured projects conceived by people who have more research grasp than they themselves appear to have, if their technical skills are to yield useful knowledge.

Readers will not be surprised that over the last twelve years I have pulled my punches a bit on these views because I recognise that they sound arrogant. Still, if we are after the truth, I had better now confess to holding them. I believe many more of the curriculum developers who were intelligent, self-critical, sceptical and thoughtful might have held these views if they had had the technical grasp to see that the psychometric emperors had no clothes. There were, however, only a few who could muster this. These tended to be associated with projects which lay outside the main academic teaching subjects of the school: the Humanities Project, the Keele Integrated Studies project and the Design and Craft Project, for instance. (They would not appoint a craft teacher to lead a project like that until he had become a Professor of Education!)

So much for the development of evaluation at the time when I entered the curriculum field. The notion of the developer as an enthusiastic reformer was certainly shared by the funding agencies, even if they did not want to tie an evaluator to his tail. They were more interested in reform than research. It was the temper of the times. Yet the Humanities Curriculum Project was, by definition (see Schools Council Working Paper no. 2), so unlikely to succeed in the terms generally accepted by the enthusiasts, that, in accepting its directorship, I made it clear that I needed the right to fail. I think the Council thought I was teasing them. Their reaction was rather to say: 'Hush, hush, you'll pull it off all right.'

In short, the picture of the curriculum project as a band of enthusiasts bent on recasting the world to their vision - the picture painted by Wiseman and Pidgeon in their little book - was widely disseminated. I believe this was a strong influence which contributed to the fact that, when we advertised for posts on the project, we got no applicants with research experience. Ours was a project which turned people into researchers, but it recruited none.

It was primarily to strengthen the research side of a research and development project which from the outset declared insistently that it was a research project that I wrote a proposal to the Schools Council, for an 'evaluation'. I asked for a Schools Study Officer to case-study schools during the trial period of the project with a view to designing an evaluation for execution at the time when the project should diffuse into the system on publication.

A paper written for our consultative committee in February 1968 illustrates the research stance of the project and the initial adumbration of the role of the evaluation.

> "Evaluation must . . . be based upon the close analytic scrutiny of the classroom. This is made technically possible by video-tape, but it will take time to make progress with the theoretical work involved in analysis.
> One great advantage of the decision to face the complexity of the classroom situation in attempting evaluation is that the case-study materials we shall be using to evaluate our work will also be broadly descriptive of our trial schools.
> This paper has attempted to define a position as clearly and precisely as possible, but it must be emphasised that this position has at the moment only the status of a hypothesis. The definition is not that of assertion. It is an attempt at the precision which makes it easier rather than more difficult to modify a position in the light of experience."

The Schools Council agreed to support the proposal put to them and I was fortunate in being able to persuade my former colleague, Barry MacDonald, to accept the post of Schools Study Officer and later that of Director of evaluation, which he himself had designed and submitted as a proposal to the Council. It is worth stressing that Barry MacDonald designed what would now be called an 'illuminative' evaluation without contact with Parlett and Hamilton and with only tenuous contacts with American evaluators. He was alone: the community came later.

He made an immense contribution to what I have called elsewhere the 'new wave' evaluation. However, our project and our centre ran into political difficulties and these excluded Barry MacDonald from another chance at a classic curriculum evaluation, as they excluded me from another chance at a curriculum project from the Schools Council. Thus, he did not really have a chance to consolidate his contribution in that field. Instead, the force of circumstances have led him and many other contemporary evaluators out of curriculum evaluation towards the evaluation of policies, institutions, and educational programmes which are not conceived as curriculum research and development.

The way was, in fact, prepared for this development in the evaluation of the Humanities Curriculum Project which, as it went on, left more room in the classroom for the project team, and extended its interests into the problems of the process of implementing curriculum experiments – or of innovation – in the schools and the school system. My own belief is that one important strand of the evaluation developed research into problems of action in the educational system. I am sceptical whether the banner of evaluation is any more than a flag of convenience for this valuable research work.

Indeed, it may at times be a flag of inconvenience, making reports more difficult to clear because they appear to be evaluations of actors rather than research into the difficulties of action. But that is another story, and I want to keep curriculum evaluation in my sights.

As a matter of fact there has been remarkably little curriculum evaluation in this country in proportion to the investment in curriculum research and development. I think that the sponsors of curriculum development have felt that evaluation is a luxury not essential for the improvement of schooling by means of work in the curriculum field. I want to argue that in principle their view is correct. There is little place for evaluation in curriculum research and development, given an adequate training for curriculum workers. But, since it is difficult to get an adequate training as a curriculum worker, there may be a need for trained research personnel to work in curriculum teams. When evaluation has been most successful in curriculum (e.g. in Science 5 to 13, and to a considerable extent in the Humanities Project), the evaluators have in fact taken this role.

This general account of my background experience and standpoint will, I hope, serve to make the analysis I now offer both more comprehensible and more accessible to criticism.

Let me look first at the crudest conception of curriculum, in which a curriculum is conceived as a set of teaching materials supported by teacher handbooks concerned mainly with use of these materials and the assessment of pupils' work. The adoption of such a curriculum is seen as a policy alternative (in this country for the school or the L.E.A.) and the choice of the curriculum is assumed to rest on its being better - in some way that we need not here define - than the alternative at present in force in the school. The most common interpretation of 'better' in the literature seems to rest on the idea of a rapidly changing world implying rapidly changing knowledge and the consequent need for updating in the school. This notion of keeping up with the times seems to be the one which originally gave life to the concept of innovation being associated with curriculum, though this concept has now been refined and has acquired sounder empirical reference.

This is a conception of curriculum which I think is quite unacceptable as the basis for curriculum research and development. It is essential that curriculum research and development treat curriculum as problematic, and any given curriculum as a means towards understanding that problems.

The first mental step that needs to be taken is to see the existing curriculum in a problematic light. We know that existing curricula falsify knowledge in the attempt to make it acceptable to learners, and to make them amenable to teaching, and that even after this distortion in knowledge to help them in their tasks educational establishments are far from successful in making their knowledge accessible to all pupils. There are of course other problematics in the relationship of curriculum to social and political power and to social class. The current curriculum is thus a failure, though in saying this one must remember that education, like most worthwhile enterprises, is an impossible task. Moreover the problems of educational change are themselves transformed by social change so that if we should ever threaten to overtake them, they would accelerate beyond our grasp. It would be easy to be less successful than we are, it is difficult to improve, yet, since it is impossible to stand still, we must struggle for improvement because failure to do so promises certain deterioration. Curriculum research and development is part of the perpetual struggle in educational research to improve schooling rather than to study its deterioration.

An important feature of this perspective on education is that it suggests that education is always an experiment and always an unsuccessful one. This means that children in a sense are always guinea pigs and that we are concerned with the problem of discriminating between worthwhile and intelligent shortfalls and failures and those shortfalls and failures which are not worthwhile or reasonably defenisble. I want to argue that the shortfalls or failures which are worthwhile are those from which pupils and teachers learn most. And indeed, if we are considering institutionalised curriculum research and development, those from which project directors learn most! And evaluators! And part of the learning comes from the capacity to treat the curriculum as hypothetical or provisional.

A curriculum is an expression in practice of a complex of hypotheses about the nature of learning in institutional and inter-personal situations and about the nature of what is to be learnt. A straightforward way to see what I mean by this is to look at Griffin's attempt to translate the educational ideas of John Dewey into a history curriculum. This work is reported in Metcalf's article on social science curricula in Gage's Handbook of Research on Teaching. Another straightforward case is that of MAN: a course of study which claims to be a translation into educational practice of ideas previously expressed in book form by Jerome Bruner. The curriculum specification in such cases provides a practitioner with a vantage point from which he can handle the critical interaction between educational ideas and educational proposals and the critical interaction between these proposals and day-to-day practice. It is possible that the students as well as the teacher will learn more because of the teachers' intelligent exploration through the curriculum of ideas about teaching and knowledge; but the question is obviously raised whether children should be encouraged to treat the curriculum as problematic as a means of maximising their learning. In cases where there is a professional researcher and developer involved, clearly he too needs to be reflective and self-critical and to maintain, like the teacher and perhaps the pupil, a second-order view of his first order actions as researcher and developer.

In fact, I seem to be saying that the worthwhile curriculum enterprise will always have as its title something like 'The justification, the possibilities, the problems and the effects of . . . teaching about controversial issues to adolescents, teaching Design and Craft, teaching Chemistry' or whatever; and the function of curriculum research and development, as of curriculum initiatives taken by teachers, ought to be seen not as some externalised kind of innovation, but as part of the natural process of the improvement of the art of teaching through a progressively more intelligent definition of the situation, and a refinement in the practice of the art which responds to that definition. The school, like the theatrical company or the orchestra, reinterprets the received and digests the new by the interpretation of it, and thus it develops its art. Shakespeare or Beethoven are reworked, contemporary plays and music which question the received tradition are met as challenges and digested.

This characterisation of curriculum research and development is no more than a suggested sketch, but it already makes clear the notion that curriculum is the medium of a kind of action research in which the hypothetical status of the curriculum can be used to ask either curricular questions or questions about the context in which curricula are acted out. Thus a curriculum research may be the best medium not only for a critique of Chemistry as a school subject, but also for getting a critical grasp on, say, the epistemological assumptions of the school or its authority structure as these are illuminated by the attempt to change Chemistry teaching. This is very clear in the case of the Humanities Curriculum Project where Schools Council Working Paper no. 2 not only suggested why it might be tried but also hypothesised why it might be difficult to bring it off.

In short curriculum research is action research. It requires a creative grasp of the subject or object of the teaching which will be involved, but it requires also a profound curiosity or spirit of enquiry into the problems of making the cultural resources of our society available to people through regular courses of study in specialised educational institutions.

Now, so long as this view of curriculum is seen as idiosyncratic, and so long as people are encouraged to embark on new curriculum enterprises in a spirit of reformist zeal, rather than of hungry enquiry, then we need evaluators and we need them badly. In short the case for the curriculum evaluator rests upon the character of the curriculum researcher approximating that ascribed to him by Wiseman and Pidgeon. But I argue that the day of the curriculum developer ought to be over. We know enough now to insist that he be a curriculum researcher. And you cannot be a researcher without being an evaluator. The curriculum researcher designs his curriculum to test hypotheses, that is to evaluate them! And that evaluation must be his responsiblity.

Thus, if I were to embark on a major curriculum project which, like the Humanities Project, allowed for a team large enough for an allocation of function among individuals, I would certainly be looking for the skills of the evaluator in the team. But in so far as these skills were to be deployed to document or measure the possibilities, problems and effects of the curriculum, in the schools, then as Director of the project I should want overall control of the evaluators. The evaluative element is an integral part of my research design. The danger of independent evaluation is that by creating a territory in which the evaluator holds that he has rights – and often exclusive rights – it discourages, or even excludes, research responses by other members of the project team. Although there may be room for specialised consultant services within a curriculum project team, there is, apart from this, no room for members who are not engaged in evaluation.

The illusion of the independent evaluation is the illusion of positivist social science that there can be some independent and disengaged view of truth. No evaluator is any more 'independent' than is a curriculum researcher.

The crucial point is this. In a curriculum research and development team inclined to develop its research stance by treating the curriculum project as action research, a tension between the curriculum worker and evaluator is inclined to develop. But this tension is not, as Wiseman and Pidgeon visualize it, between the impatient actor and the critical researcher. It is a tension between two similarly motivated groups of people about possession of data and the right to publish accounts or evaluative assessments of the Project. In short I believe that the existence of an independent evaluation of the Humanities Project impeded me in reporting on it as a research project and also prevented me from insisting that the evaluators should do so. And I regret that.

In a way it is the new wave evaluators who, by destroying the notion of an objective assessment of curriculum, have created the methods that make it possible to think of curriculum research and development in this way. And the success of the HCP evaluators was that they contributed strongly to making the project team want to evaluate.

The justification for the existence of curriculum research and development as a notion separate from teaching is that its concern is to design curricula for the purpose of research. In this context there is no case for an independent evaluator unless the project is indequately designed. And if the project is inadequately designed, then the remedy is rather to find the right person to redesign the proejct that to attempt to deal with the difficulty by appointing an evaluator.

In addressing the issues of the justification, the possibilities, the problems and the effects of curricular action in schools there is no place for the independent evaluator. The evaluator should be made responsible to - or, if you like, should be -the project director.

But there remains of course the problem of the accountability of the person involved in funded curriculum research and development. And certainly here, as a project director, I would be happy to have an evaluator or auditor or project historian whose task it was to look critically at the conduct of the project both in respect of its internal management and its management of its contacts with the system. These are areas in which the project is almost bound to find itself committed to actions which are not motivated by a spirit of enquiry. And indeed the advantage of such an evaluation or audit would be that the inclusion of evaluation in the responsiblity of the project would give the auditor/evaluator the right to evaluate the evaluation. It is my conviction that those who at present practice curriculum evaluation would benefit more from accountability than from independence. Indeed, if they were more accountable for their own conduct in research terms and for its productivity, they would be in a better position to assert its political independence.

A footnote of regret. I started from contextualising Wiseman and Pidgeon's approach to evaluation in the politics of educational research. With the institutionalisation of 'new wave' evaluation, I think we have produced a situation in which there is some danger that evaluators create their own establishment and glamorize it as an elite. Let's keep hold of the idea that it is mostly a matter of commonsense and learning from experience. That is not entirely true but it keeps us from going technical and theological; and a little modest oversimplification is better than a lapse into jargon or pretentiousness.

REFERENCES

Gage, N. Handbook of Research on Teaching. Schools Council Working
    Paper No. 2.
Schools Council (1965) Working Paper No. 2. Raising the School
    Leaving Age.
Wiseman, Stephen and Pidgeon, Douglas A. (1970) Curriculum
    Evaluation. N.F.E.R. Slough.

GUIDELINES I

Guidelines for the Conduct of an Independent Evaluation

Helen Simons

Introduction

This short paper outlines one set of guidelines that were used in the conduct and dissemination of an independent evaluation of a curriculum project which involved a number of 'interested parties' at different levels in the educational system. Other settings may necessitate different procedures though the principles, I think, have general relevance for evaluations that aspire to independent conduct and reporting.

Principles and Procedures of the Evaluation

The evaluation was conducted according to the principles of independence, impartiality, confidentiality, and consultation. The rationale for selecting these principles is briefly outlined before listing the specific procedures, based on these principles, which were followed in practice.

Independence

One purpose of evaluation of a publicly-funded project is to provide data to inform policy-making, another is to make the experience of the project accessible to different audiences - to all those who have a right to knowledge about the programme. The principle of independence is intended to safeguard the evaluation against the pressure of different interest groups and to ensure that the evaluation reports can be disseminated to all legitimate audiences. The major procedural problem is how to make evaluation information accessible to different groups without advocating the interests of any one.

Impartiality

The principle of impartiality is supportive to the principle of independence but is different from it. It requires the evaluator to check accounts for bias and to secure fair and 'objective' reporting.

Confidentiality

Confidentiality is necessary to protect individuals from inappropriate use of information which is private to them. Rules of access and consultation give individuals opportunities to decide what to share, to reflect on what they have shared, to edit or comment upon their information in context: to control, in other words, the use of their own information.

Consultation

Consultation, as already indicated, is a complementary principle of the principle of confidentiality. It is important at three levels. First, access to evaluation information should be sought not assumed. Secondly, if personal information (private facts of judgements) is given in confidence and that information proves relevant for the evaluation, the evaluator should consult with the person who gave the information to see if he/she will allow that information to go on public record. Thirdly, if information is not given in confidence (i.e. given with full permission for its use and therefore on public record) the evaluator should still try to allow the person opportunitities to check that the information he/she offered has been used properly in context.

The balance between these principles is a delicate one. Ideally they complement and interact to produce an accurate, fair and relevant evaluation which respects both the privacy of individuals and the public's right to know. Different principles may assume priority at particular stages of the evaluation but they should not be used to contradict each other. Use of any one principle to the exclusion of another would be an improper use – against the canons of responsible evaluation. The principle of confidentiality, for instance, while necessary to protect an individual's right to control their own information, is not a restrictive principle for all data at all times. Some data is already on the public record; some data which exists should be part of the public record; some data needs to become part of the public record. The principle cannot legitimately be invoked to prevent relevant information being reported in a publicly funded project. Such an interpretation of the principle would effectively curtail the conduct of any independent evaluation and prohibit information pertinent to an understanding of the programme in action becoming publicly accessible.

Because the balance required is a delicate one the procedures outlined below were rigorously followed in practice to protect individuals' rights to privacy, to give them the right of representation and to ensure accurate, fair and public reporting.

Procedures

Independence
-      No participants had privileged access to the data of the evaluation or the evaluation report (see Consultation).

- Decision on circulation of the evaluation report were the responsibility of the evaulator, but the fullest consultation was entered into with participants prior to circulation (see Consultation).

- There was no secret reporting or leakage or information, i.e. reports or information about individuals of which they were not aware and which had not been negotiated for fairness, accuracy and relevance.

- Circulation of reports was restricted initially to those groups whom the report concerned; once information had been checked by participants and they had been given sufficient time to add or amend comments, the report was considered ready for circulation to other legitimate agents.

- No one individual or group had the right to limit the circulation of the total evaluation.

- No one individual or group had the right to control information which was public knowledge.

Impartiality

- No fact was included that did not have at least two data sources.

- Information was crosschecked several times for accuracy, with different people, with available documents and in meetings.

- The issues reported were those identified as central at the time by the majority of participants.

- The evaluator aspired to represent all views fairly; differences of view were regarded as data to be communicated, not matters on which the evaluator arbitrated.

- The evaluator adopted the role of documenting events and perceptions accurately and fairly.

- The evaluation is non-recommendatory, i.e. the evaluator does not recommend or prescribe what should happen on the basis of the events described. Data is presented to provide a range of perspectives on issues, to inform decisions, to raise options, and to draw attention to unconsidered phenomena. (This approach assures participants that their decisions will not be pre-empted.)

- The evaluator does not have a vested interest in the subject under investigation.

- The evaluator asked an evaluation colleague to check the report for evaluation bias. The colleague also adhered to the principle of confidentiality.

Confidentiality

- Interviews and informal conversations were confidential to the individual if requested.

  The evaluator did not use any information (oral or written) given to the evaluator in confidence without his/her consent.

- It was explained to individuals before the interview as to how the information would be used, viz. - that judgments and perspectives individuals wanted to keep private would be respected:

  - that individuals would have the opportunity to see the report and check the use of the information in context and to add any further comments they thought appropriate;

  - that if the evaluator wished to use specific quotations in the evaluation, permission would be sought from the individual;

  - that individuals would have an opportunity to reflect upon and check any other comments they made which formed part of the narrative on general issues;

  - that permission would not be sought from individuals for the use of information which did not identify them or which was already shared general knowledge.

  - that the individual would have the opportunity to see and comment upon the report before circulation to other groups.

- Individuals had total control over information which was private to them and which they expressly asked to be kept in confidence.

- No one individual or group had the right to control information which was shared, i.e. not confidential to them only or which others cleared through the process of consultation.

- Respect for confidentiality was maintained: where a person said "Don't quote me" the quotation was not used; where a person said "Can you say that indirectly?"" the comment was rephrased; where a person said "Can you make that point in a general way?" an attempt was made to do so.

- Where individuals are described pseudonyms or roles are used in the report. While this does not assure anonymity from those in the immediate environment, it decreases the probability of identification over time and distance.

Consultation
- Access to data sources was negotiated with those responsible. Data sources included head teachers, teachers, pupils, parents, local district personnel, project team, project records, school records and public statements, examples of pupils' work, teaching materials, etc. Where appropriate, permission for the use of information relevant to the evaluation from those data sources was also sought from the same individuals.

- Permission for the use of information given in confidence which proved relevant for the evaluation was sought from the individuals concerned.

- Interviews, discussions, group meetings, written statements were all potential data for the evaluation; but individuals had the opportunity to check the accuracy of the reportage, to correct or improve attributable interview statements to suggest amendments.

- The evaluator negotiated aspects of the reports which concerned particular individuals with them on the criteria of fairness, accuracy and relevance.

- Key individuals who contributed to the evaluation and who were identifiable in the report, even in role, had the opportunity to comment on the sections which concerned them (checking specific attributable quotations and points of view) before the report was circulated to the group as a whole; numerous amendments were made by participants and these have been incorporated into the text.

- The same individuals had the further opportunity to comment on the issues when the report was released to the group as a whole. Comments were invited on the criteria of accuracy, fairness and relevance and an assurance given by the evaluator to amend the report in the light of these comments and to include any additional statements which participants thought necessary. A fortnight was given initially,but this was extended to six weeks to allow more time for the preparation of a statement which the local district group indicated that they wished to make. Two project teachers each made further comments which have been included in the text.

- Secondly, the report was disseminated to the other group of key individuals -head teachers - with the same invitation to comment on the criteria of fairness, accuracy and relevance and the same assurance to amend or include any additional comments. No comments were received.

- The report was then disseminated (via the head teachers) to the class teachers from whose classes pupils were withdrawn for the project and to the middle and upper school heads whose schools were involved in the project but who were not directly reported upon in the evaluation; and then to two evaluation consultants and the college. The local district had decided by this stage not to make a response.

- One month later the report was disseminated to the European Community and their Comparative Evaluation Team.

Dissemination

The report was disseminated in phases according to the following principles:

- That those most closely involved in the project and who are identifiable in the report, even by role alone, should receive the report first and have the opportunity to comment upon it before circulation to the other groups involved.

- That head teachers whose schools are involved should, similarly, have the opportunity to comment on the report before circulation to the class teachers and the sponsoring groups.

- That those class teachers whose contribution to the report and whose pupils are involved should have the report for information and to further understanding of the issues involved.

- That other class teachers and the two heads whose schools were not directly reported upon should receive the report for information and understanding of the issues.

- That the sponsoring groups should have access to the evaluation to further their understanding of the issues involved in setting up and implementing such projects.

- That other 'interested parties' should have access to the report once it has been through the above procedures and stages, to further their understanding of the issues involved in such projects.

GUIDELINES II

What can be said; what must be said; the Evaluator, the Law of Defamation and Privilege generally

Ann McAllister

Introduction

Anyone carrying out evaluation or research, particularly into the suitability and performance of certain people in their work, runs the risk of inadvertently straying into the complex area of the law known as defamation - a term which includes both libel and slander. Inadvertently because defamation does not depend on any intent to defame - the test is a purely objective one: would a right thinking person say that such a statement tends to lower the plaintiff in the esteem of right thinking people? So in general any imputation which casts doubts on someone's ability to teach or suggests that for moral or other reasons they may not be suited for their post is prima facie a defamation. Of course, if the defamatory statement was not actuated by what in law is known as malice the level of damages that might otherwise be awarded to the plaintiff will be substantially reduced. But it is not for the plaintiff to prove that the statement was untrue; he or she is entitled to a good name unless the contrary is proved.

Equally clearly there can be no defamation if the statement made is substantially true. This is known as the defence of justification. It has to be proved on a balance of probabilities and it is a complete defence which holds good even if it can be shown that the defendant was actually motivated by spite, or ill-will or any other improper motive.

More important for evaluators or researchers (as well as for teachers generally) are the defences of fair comment and qualified privilege. For these, it is not essential to prove the truth of the statement, only a relevant and honest comment, but the defences will in turn be defeated if it can be shown that the defendant knew the statement to be untrue or had some ulterior motive. They afford some protection, in other words, to what might be described as the negligent or careless defamer. As their ambit is very wide, it can almost be said, particularly with reference to evaluators or researchers, that those defences turn the law of defamation on its head.

Fair comment means that an opinion, as long as honestly held and as long as it concerns a matter of public interest, can be expressed with impunity even it exaggerated or unreasonable so long as the facts to which it refers are true and made clear. If someone is convicted of assaulting children it is ordinarily a fair comment to say that he or she is unfit to teach. Again, comments on insanitary conditions in schools would come within this category. Indeed, anything that concerns a school is likely to be a matter of public interest.

Justification and fair comment are defences which are available to all. Qualified privilege depends essentially on a relationship of reciprocity between the person making the statement and the person receiving it: the maker must be under a duty (legal, social or moral) to make the statement and the other person to receive it; or there must be some common interest; or there must be a relationship of trust and reliance. A report by an evaluator or researcher would generally be covered by qualified privilege: the reporter is under a duty to report what he or she sees and learns, and indeed teachers or heads may be under a duty to report to an evaluator or researcher what they know of fellow teachers or other members of staff. Similarly reports, whether written or spoken, by teachers about pupils, as well as testimonials and references, and reports made about teachers by parents or pupils to the local education authority, or to the head of the school will prima facie attract qualified privilege. Codes of practice regarding whether or not such reports should be shown to the person they concern are not relevant to the law of defamation. If the defendant can show that the communication was privileged, the onus then shifts back to the plaintiff to prove malice, that is to prove an improper motive. Generally, if the plaintiff can show that the defendant knew the statement to be untrue he or she wil succeed.

Another problem which may face a researcher is the problem of what must be disclosed in any court proceedings in which he or she is a party or a witness. To what extent must his or her findings and conclusions be made known? Can a researcher be compelled to give evidence? One may be involved for instance in a case where a teacher is contesting dismissal.

In essence there is no shield of confidentiality to protect what has passed between researcher and informant (any more than there is between doctor and patient or journalist and source); nor, it apears, will confidentiality be protected by a wider cloak of public interest except where criminal information needs shielding. So a relevant and necessary question put in court must be answered even if answering involves breaking confidence.

The subsequent sections of this chapter may be of substantial interest to those who want to know why the law says what it does, but readers should be warned that they cannot resolve any problem of defamation or privileged evidence which actually arises simply by reference to this chapter: they should seek a lawyer's advice.

English law of defamation rests on the premise that every man is entitled to his good name and to the esteem in which he is held by others and will afford him protection if his reputation is disparaged by defamatory statements made about him to a third party without lawful justification or excuse. Two separate civil actions ,[1] the action of libel and the action of slander, are provided by law. Libel may also be a criminal offence because of its tendency to provoke a breach of the peace.[2]

Broadly speaking if a defamatory statement is made in writing or printing or in some other permanent form the tort of libel is committed and the law will presume that the publication has caused damage to the plaintiff: he need not, in other words, prove that he has suffered damage to establish a cause of action. If the defamatory statement, on the other hand, is oral or in some other fugitive form the plaintiff, in order to establish the tort of slander, must further prove either that the words are actionable per se or that he has suffered special damage.[3] It should further be noted that defamatory matter which is broadcast in a radio or television programme for general reception will be treated as libel as will generally be the publication of defamatory matter on the stage.[4] The distinction between libel and slander (which is undoubtedly partly responsible for the undue complexity and technicality of the law of defamation generally) is difficult to justify on any logical or juridical principle and rests largely on the historical development of this area of the law.[5]

In order to establish a prima facie case in an action either for libel or slander the plaintiff must prove that the words were defamatory of him and that they were published of, and concerned the plaintiff.[6]

There is no complete, comprehensive or indeed statutory definition of what consitutes a defamatory statement.[7] The essence of such a statement is its tendency to injure the reputation of another person. In particular it will be defamatory if it tends to lower the plaintiff in the estimation of right thinking members of society generally[8] or it exposes him to public hatred contempt or ridicule or if it causes him to be shunned and avoided. And, of particular relevance to the researcher, it has been held that words will be defamatory if they impute lack of qualification, knowledge, skill, capacity, judgement or efficiency in the conduct of the plaintiff's trade, business or professional activity. Indeed if the words complained of carry such an imputation and are spoken rather than published in some permanent form, they will found an action for slander without proof of special damage.[9] It can be seen therefore that defamation is not necessarily based on any suggestion of moral obliqity.[10] Moreover, if a reasonable person believes that the words refer to the plaintiff the defendant will not escape liability by disguising his reference to the plaintiff by using intials, ficititious names or any other subterfuge and it has been conclusively established that the intention and knowledge of the defendant are irrelevant. Thus a defendant may be liable even if he has never heard of the plaintiff or intended to refer to someone else.[11] If the plaintiff is seeking to shown that the words would be understood to refer to him because of some facts or circumstances which are extrinsic to the words themselves, he must plead and prove these facts in order to connect him with the person complained of, but again it does not matter that the extrinsic facts are unknown to those responsible for the publication of the words.[12]

Thus while in a civil action[13] for libel or slander the plaintiff must prove that the words complained of have been published to some third person (in this respect the law is not concerned merely to protect injured feelings or hurt pride - although both may be relevant to an assessment of damages - nor does English law recognise the tort of invasion of privacy) the risk of coincidence or unintended defamation clearly falls on the defendant unless as we shall see below, the defence of qualified privilege obtains.

While it is not possible therefore to formulate a water-tight definition of what is defamatory it is clear that this will depend to some extent on the occupation of the plaintiff wherever allegations of incompetence etc. are being made. (Equally clearly allegations of dishonesty or immorality or other dishonourable conduct do not depend per se on a particular occupation). It would be defamatory of a teacher to say that he or she had no aptitude for teaching just as it would be defamatory to say of an accountant that he had no understanding of figures, while such allegations would not be defamatory if made of persons whose business or profession did not require such skills.

In Drummond-Jackson v British Medical Association 1970 1 WLR 688 the Court of Appeal examined an article in a medical journal which, according to the plaintiff, impugned his reputation as a dentist by launching a severe attack on a technique for preserving teeth which was associated with him. The majority of the court held (Lord Denning dissenting) that it would be open to the jury to conclude that this did indeed involve an attact on his reputation as a dentist and was therefore capable of bearing a meaning defamatory to the plaintiff. (The court was not at this stage concerned with whether any defence such as that of justification or fair comment would be open to the defendant). In McCarogher v Franks 1964 CLY 2137 the plaintiff, a school-teacher, claimed damages for slander against the defendant who was secretary of the Old Boys' Association alleging that he had told some pupils that she was abnormal and that 'women of her age were often like that'. The words were held to be defamatory, but the defendant succeeded on a plea of qualified privilege. And again in Butler v Oz Publications, reported in the Times of the 30th of June 1972 the defendant publication alleged that the plaintiff a teacher, 'liked caning people'. The Defendants withdrew the imputation and expressed their sincere apologies for the embarrassement they may have caused, thus admitting the defamatory nature of the words. Cases in other jurisdictions provide further illustrations of what may be defamatory when said or written of a school-teacher.[14]

Having proved that the words in question were published of the plaintiff and defamatory of him, the plaintiff will further have to prove that there was a publication of the words complained of, that is, a communication of those words to some person other than the plaintiff.[15] In a libel action, publication consists in making known the defamatory statement after it has been reduced to some permanent form:[16] merely to write dwon the words is not to publish a libel, nor is there any publication if the third party does not become aware of the defamatory words. Again, if the writer of a letter or a report locks it in his own desk and a third party breakes it open and makes its contents known, that would not be publication by the writer. In an action for slander, a person publishes a slander who speaks words defamatory of the plaintiff to or in the presence of a third person who hears them and understands them in a defamatory sense. There is authority for the preposition that mere dictation of a defamatory matter to a typist is the publication of a slander while the reading of such a matter, knowing it to be defamatory, to any person other than the person defamed is the publication of a libel.[17]

The burden of proving that the words were published to a third party rests as we have seen on the plaintiff. In some cases, however, publication is presumed, for instance were publication takes place in a book or newspaper or public broadcast, and if this is the case there is no need for the plaintiff to prove that the words were published to any specific person or persons.

Every person who publishes (in the sense of making known, as explained above) or causes to be published or participates in a publication is liable as a publisher. Thus, to take the obvious example of a libel appearing in a newspaper, the author of the libel, the proprietor, editor, printer, publisher and vendor (the latter subject to the defence of innocent dissemination) will all be liable. But to dissiminate innocently a defamatory document is not to publish it: so a postman who delivers a letter without knowing of its contents, or a librarian, bookseller, newsvendor who in the ordinary course of business circulates or sells a book without knowing that it contains defamatory matter and without being negligent in not so knowing are not liable. The onus of proving innocent dissemination lies on the person seeking to establish it.

Lastly, on the subject of publication, is the question of the liability of the original publisher on re-publication. _Prima facie_, a person who publishes a libel is not liable for its unauthorised and voluntary republication by the person to whom he first published it. But he will be liable if the authorised or intended the repetition; if there was an obligation on the other person to repeat the words (whether legal or moral) and probably where the repetition was the natural consequence of the publication by the original publisher.[18]

It may be appropriate at this point to recapitulate what has been said so far about the ingredients necessary to found an action for slander or libel. We have seen that there must be a defamatory statement, that this must, for a civil action, be published to a third party, and that it must concern the plaintiff. Some of the issues raised by this last ingredient, notably the question of identifying the plaintiff, were discussed above. But what is the situation if the words complained of contain defamatory allegations against a group of people, for instance, teachers in general, or the teachers of a particular subject, or of a particular school? If the group is one to which the Race Relations Act applies an action may exist by virtue of that enactment, but a class of persons cannot be defamed as a class, nor can an individual be defamed by a general reference to the class to which he belongs unless he can show that, notwithstanding the fact that the statement reflected on a group of persons, he was personally pointed to or aimed at by the words. Thus if the language used in reference to a limited group can be reasonably understood to refer to every member of that group, every member will have a cause of action.[19] The question is not whether the words were spoken of a group of class, but whether they were spoken of the plaintiff. As Lord Atkin said:[20]

> 'There can be no law that a defamatory statement made of a firm, or trustees or the tenants of a particular building is not actionable, if the words would reasonably be understood as published of each member of the firm or each trustee or each tenant'.

An important factor in deciding whether the words complained of refer to the plaintiff is the size of the class of which he is a member. To say 'all teachers' are 'incompetent' may make it difficult for any particular teacher to prove that the words referred to him. But there are judicial dicta[21] suggesting that a member of even a large class may have a cause of action: this might be the case if it is alleged that 'to become a teacher you must have committed a murder', to take an exagerrated example. The smaller the group of people referred to, the easier it will be for any individual plaintiff to show that the words referred to him. 'The maths teachers like caning' when there are only three teachers may be reasonably understood as referring to each of them, and each will have the right of action. In each instance it will be question of fact whether or not reasonable persons reading or hearing the words would understand them to point to the particular plaintiff.

Having thus looked at the ingredients for an action of libel or slander the next, and crucial, topic is that of possible defences to an action for defamation. Clearly, the defendant may contend that the plaintiff is unable to prove a prima facie case, either because the words complained of were not published at all or were not published by him, or because the words did not and could not be understood to be referring to the plaintiff or because the words were not defamatory. This is merely another way of saying that the tort of libel or slander has not been made out. In addition to this, the law provides a number[22] of defences which may be raised to defeat the plaintiffs claim once a prima facie case is made out.

Of particular note in the present context are the defences of justification, fair comment, and privilege, whether absolute or qualified.

The essence of justification is that the words complained of are true in substance and in fact. The burden of proof is on the defendant. If the words are true it is quite irrelevant that the words were published with the express intent of causing damage to the plaintiff.[23] To satisfy the burden of proof the defendant must show that the 'sting of the charge' is true: he need not prove every detail, but the substance of the matters alleged. If the words amount to a general charge or allegation (e.g. X is a bad teacher) it is not enough to show that on a specific instance he has shown himself to be such, and if the defendant is relying on rumour or hearsay he must prove the truth of the subject matter of the rumour, not merely that the rumour existed.[24] On the other hand if the words complained of contain more than one charge or can in any event be severed the defendant may justify part only of the words. In this case, he remained liable at common law for the part he had not justified. So that if the defendant says of someone that 'he is a homosexual and a thief', he may be able to justify one only of those charges, and be liable for the other. The defence of partial justification has been extended by statute and may in certain circumstances afford a complete defence. By s 5 of the Defamation Act 1952 where there is an action for libel or slander in respect of words containing two or more distinct charges against the plaintiff, a defence of justification shall not fail by reason only that the truth of every charge is not proved, if the words not proved to be true do not materially injure the plaintiff's reputation having regard to the truth of the remaining charges. Justification or 'truth' as it might be more appropriately called[25] is based on the rationale that a man should not be entitled to recover damages in respect of an injury to a character which he does not or ought not to possess: if he has no reputation to lose nothing that can be said about him will lower him in the eyes of right thinking people. The defence of fair comment, on the other hand, is predicated on somewhat less simple grounds. To state accurately and truthfully what a man has done and then comment adversely on it may not do a great deal of harm since everyone can judge for themselves and draw whatever inference may be appropriate from that behaviour, whereas a mistatement of facts leaves no room for independent judgement. Accordingly, it will be a defence if the defendant can prove that the matter on which he was commenting was one of public interest, that the comment was based on fact while remaining recognisable as comment, that any man might honestly have expressed such an opinion on the known facts and that the plaintiff cannot succeed in proving that the defendant was actuated by express malice.

As to what is public interest, even though there is no exhaustive definition, case law clearly shows[26] that it encompasses a very wide field indeed. It is enough that the matter should affect people at large even though it may only directly concern a small number of people.[27] There is no doubt that any matter relating to the management of a school or to the behaviour of teachers acting in their professional role would fall within this ambit. The comment in question must further be based on facts which are either stated or indicated by the person making the comment so as to allow the reader or listener to distinguish between what is comment and what is not. Again it is necessary to prove that all the facts stated as the basis for the comment are true, (unless the stated facts are protected by privilege, see below), subject to section 6 of the Defamation Act 1952.[28] In order to qualify as fair comment, the expression of opinion must satisfy the following objective test: could any man honestly express that opinion of the proved facts? However prejudiced or obstinate he might be? The question to be answered by the jury is not 'do you agree with what he said?', but 'could a fair minded man holding strong views, obstinate views, prejudiced views have been capable of making this comment?'[29] The scope of the defence of fair comment in relation to an imputation of corrupt, dishonourable or dishonest motive is not altogether clear, but despite authority to the contrary[30] the better view seems to be that such an imputation can be defended as fair comment provided it is put forward as an honest expression of opinion. Lastly, it must be noted that even though the comment satisfies the objective test of fair comment, the defence will still fail if the plaintiff proves that express malice actuated the defendant in making the comment. A comment tinged with malice cannot by definition be a fair one. In essence malice (which will be examined further below) means that the defendant had an improper motive for publishing the comment and that this improper motive was the sole or dominant motive.

We turn now to the defence of privilege. Privilege can be of two sorts: absolute or qualified. In the context of this paper, qualified privilege is of the utmost importance. In outline this means that although the defamatory comments are not true the publisher will be protected if the statements are made in persuance of a duty (whether legal or moral) or for the protection of a common interest with the person to whom they were made as long as, once again, the defendant was not actuated by express malice. Generally the fact that he did not believe what he was saying will be conclusive evidence of such malice. If the defence is made out the effect is to shift the risk of unintended injury to reputation to the plaintiff: the state of the defendant's mind is thus crucial.

Before examining qualified privilege in greater detail, a word must be said about absolute privilege. As the adjective implies, if the occasion is absolutely privileged no action for defamation lies, whether or not the defendant was actuated by express malice. Precisely because it offers complete protection, even to the unscrupulous, the ambit of this defence is narrow. The occasions of absolute privilege can be classified as the administration of justice (i.e. statements made in judicial or quasi judicial proceedings), proceedings in Parliament, certain aspects of local government administration, statements made by one officer of State to another in the course of duty – in all these cases it is felt that it is in the interest of the public that persons speaking or writing in or about those occasions, if they fall within certain categories, should be permitted to express themselves with complete freedom. An individual's reputation can thus be sacrificed to the common good. Of particular relevance here are statements made in the ordinary course of proceedings before any court or any tribunal exercising functions equivalent to those of an established court of justice whether made in the course of the trial or hearing or in the course of proceedings which are essential steps towards such a trial or hearing. Not every tribunal is protected by absolute privilege: to be so, it must be recognised by law, its object must be to arrive at a judicial determination and it must proceed in a manner similar to a court of justice. In Trapp v Mackie (1979) 1 WLR 377 the appellant was dismissed from the post of headmaster. A local inquiry was held before a commissioner appointed by the Secretary of State under section 81 (3) of the Education (Scotland) Act 1946, in the course of which the respondent gave evidence. The question, ultimately before the House of Lords, was whether the respondent's comments were protected by absolute privilege. Lord Diplock, giving a careful and considered judgement, found that they were. The tribunal in this instance was acting in a way (that is sufficiently close a court of justice) that it was right that it would attract absolute privilege. A very recent case[31] illustrates however that the courts are reluctant to extend this principle to conciliation hearings (even if one of the objects is to settle disputes and in so doing establish the truth) or indeed to all arbitrations.

Qualified privilege, on the other hand, is a relative defence. On grounds of public policy the law affords protection on certain occasions to a person acting in good faith and without improper motive who makes a statement about another which is in fact untrue and defamatory. Once again, there is no statutory codification of the protected occasions[32] but at common law the thread linking the occasions together is the existence of a common and corresponding duty or interest between the person making and the person receiving the statement. Unlike fair comment, the defence of privilege is in the nature of a restricted right, and can only be invoked by those defendants who have a duty to make the comments or who do so to protect a common interest.

What then is meant by statements made in persuance of a duty? Various points require to be noted. First the duty need not be a legal one, but a moral or social one. A moral duty is one recognised by English people of ordinary intelligence and moral principal, or, to put it another way, would right-minded persons in the place of the defendant have considered it their duty under the circumstances to make such a communication?[33] Secondly, the duty can either arise because information was requested from the defendant by a third party regarding the plaintiff, or may arise from the circumstances themselves, in which case the defendant will be under a duty to volunteer the information. Thirdly (and this applies also to the second category of privilege, i.e. statements made for the protection or furtherance of an interest) the statements must be made to a person who has a corresponding duty or as the case may be, interest, to receive them. Reciprocity is essential. Examples of the above duties are statements made by employers as to employees' characters, for example, references, or reports to an employment agency, or statements made to fellow employees giving the reason for the employee ceasing to be employed, as long as the fellow employee had an interest not merely in the fact of his co-worker no longer working there, but the reason for it. Similarly an employee (such as a teacher) may be under a duty to report a fellow teacher to the head of the school for drunkeness or other misbehaviour which might affect his teaching and which a reasonable person would consider it his duty to report.[34] Indeed the duty to report such matters may extend to anyone who has a legitimate interest in inquiring about the work of his colleagues - for instance, to a researcher. In certain cases, there may be a duty to volunteer the information to a researcher or to persons in authority without being asked. In this case the degree to which the defendant has taken steps to verify the truth of his statements (e.g. that X drinks too much or shows too much interest in his female pupils) may be relevant to the existence of the duty. It is not possible to give an exhaustive definition of when such a duty has been held to arise, but as it can be seen, the ambit of qualified privilege is very wide indeed. In McCarogher v Franks (see above) the statements made by the secretary of the school's Old Boys' Association were held to attract qualified privilege on the grounds of the relationship of trust and reliance between the defendant and the boys to whom he had made the defamatory comments. In Bridgeman v Stockdale 1953 1 WLR 704 it was held that an invigilator's statement to examinees that the plaintiff had cheated was privileged.

The second broad category in this area is not where someone is under a duty to make a comment, but where a comment is made by someone with an interest in the subject matter to someone who has a corresponding interest in receiving it. These distinctions, of course, between 'duty' and 'interest' have no legal significance other than in serving to illustrate the broad principle that certain communications 'in the general interest of society' should be protected as long as there is, as explained above, some reciprocity of interest - which does not mean a special relationship, but merely that the person receiving the information has an interest which is more than mere idle curiosity. In McIntyre v McBean (1866) 13 Up Can QB 534 a petition signed by the residents of a school district and addressed to the school board requesting the removal of a teacher for immorality and intemperence was held to be privileged.

Further at common law[35] reports of judicial proceedings, reports of proceedings in Parliament and of other public proceedings where the publication is for the public interest whether they are published in newspapers or elsewhere with the purpose of informing the public are similarly privileged, unless malice can be established. Again at common law this privilege was held not to extend to reports of proceedings before a domestic tribunal or any other tribunal or arbitration where the public is not entitled to be present. This also has been modified by statute.[36] The publication in a newspaper or by broadcasting of a fair and accurate report of the findings of an association formed for the purpose of promoting, inter alia, the exercise of learning and empowered to exercise control over or adjudicate upon matters of interest to the association as long as it is a finding relating to a person who is a member of that association is protected. Thus qualified privilege not only covers those situations where there is a duty to communicate a statement, or a common interest to be protected but also broadly speaking whenever a fair and accurate report is made of proceedings of a public nature. It is a question of law for the judge whether the occasion of publication is protected by qualified privilege: if it is the onus of proof shifts to the plaintiff to prove express malice. If there are disputed questions of fact upon which the existence of privilege may depend, the determiantion of those facts is for the jury. It should be emphasised that neither the absence of malice nor the mere belief on the defendant's part that the occasion was privileged is sufficient to found the defence. The question whether a defendant was motivated by a sense of duty (crucial to the question of malice) is not relevant to the question: was the occasion privileged? Nor will a communication be privileged because the person making it believed honestly but mistakenly that person receiving it had a duty or interest in receiving it, if in fact he had not. The existence or non existence of privilege in other words does not depend on the state of the defendant's mind. But once privilege is established, the state of his mind becomes of the utmost importance.

Express of actual malice, if proved, can defeat both a defence of qualified privilege and of fair comment. Malice is not limited to its colloquial usage of spite or ill will, but includes any indirect or improper motive, such as anger, jealousy or ambition. On the other hand proof of the existence of bad feeling is not the same as proof that the defendant was actuated by malice. The fact that the defendant did not believe what he said was true or was reckless as to whether it was true or not (although this must be distinguised from carelessness or impulsiveness in arriving at a positive belief in the truth of what was published) is usually conclusive evidence of malice, and will rebut the defence of qualified privilege. If fair comment is pleaded, it is usually sufficient to defeat the defence it it can be shown that the defendant did not honestly hold the opinion expressed.[37] Even where the defendant did believe the words to be true it may still be possible to prove that publication was actuated by an improper motive, for instance a desire to injure the plaintiff or to achieve some personal advantage not connected with duty or interest. Finally if irrelevant defamatory matter is included in the publication (i.e. not relevant to the subject matter attracting privilege) the proper approach is to treat such irrelevant matter as one of the factors to be taken into account in deciding whether an inference that the defendant was actuated by express malice can properly be drawn. It is then a question for the jury to decide on the balance of probabilities whether or not the defendant acted maliciously.

Lastly, in the context of defamation a word should be said about the relief to which the plaintiff is entitled on proving his case. This can either take the form of an injunction in appropriate cases to prevent the repetition of the libel or slander, or an award of damages. In the latter case, the general rule is that damages are to be assessed on a compensatory basis, taking into account, as a rule of thumb, the seriousness of the libel, any special damage, (i.e. loss which is pecuniary or capable of being estimated in money e.g. loss of employment) injury to the plaintiff's feelings, as offset by any mitigating factors. These include the reputation of the plaintiff, the plaintiff's behaviour towards the defendant, any apology tendered by the defendant and any other relevant fact. In certain restricted cases[38] exemplary or punitive damages may be awarded.

So far we have been examining the relevance of the concept of privilege in the context of the law of defamation where, as we have seen, it can be raised as a defence to an action of libel or slander. But the notion of privilege also has a part to play in the general law of evidence: it may be invoked in the course of proceedings, both criminal and civil[39] as a shield by a witness to justify his refusal to answer certain questions or to produce documentary evidence which would otherwise be relevant and hence discoverable. In this chapter, this aspect of 'privilege' will only be discussed in outline.

Firstly, three inter-related concepts need to be distinguised: that is, the competence, compellability and privilege of a witness. Generally speaking everyone is a competent witness (but note that the accused is not a competent witness for the prosecution and nor, subject to some important exceptions, is his spouse) - that is he may be lawfully called to give evidence. And whoever can be lawfully called to give evidence, can also be lawfully obliged to do so, that is he will also be a compellable witness.[40] Failure to testify can result in imprisonment.

Secondly, there are certain occasions where a witness who is both competent and compellable can refuse to answer questions or produce evidence and these are the occasions when privilege can be invoked.[41]

Fourthly relevant evidence may be excluded on the grounds of public policy when it concerns certain matters of public interest. This is known as public interest immunity. The exact limits of this latter immunity are far from clear although it can be tentatively stated that (with the possible exception of child care cases (43)) public interest in the disclosure of relevant documents wil outweigh the need for secrecy and confidentiality unless national security or other national interests are involved.

As regards the privilege against self-incrimination it is clear law that no-one is bound to answer any questions if the answer would have a tendency to expose the deponent to any criminal charge or penalty, whether in criminal or civil proceedings, unless statute provides to the contrary.[44] Legal professional privilege concerns confidential communications passing between a lawyer and his client, and in some cases extends to protect confidential communications between the lawyer or client and third parties. In the latter case, the rule is more restrictive: communications will only be privileged if they are brought into existence after litigation has started or is contemplated and the communications are made for the purpose of giving or obtaining legal advice in the litigation or for the obtaining of information and evidence for use in the litigation.[45] It would seem that such privilege cannot be extended to other relationships, for instance to priest and penitent, or doctor and patient, or indeed journalist and informer, nor to researcher and informer.[46]

We have seen that the production of documents may sometimes be refused on the ground of what is commonly referred to as public interest immunity.[47] Confidentiality (that is the need to protect documents containing the sources of information) is not a separate head of privilege, but a material consideration in establishing whether public interest demands that documents should not be disclosed. Thus protection has been afforded to statements and identity of police informers,[48] to material supplied by businessmen to the Customs and Excise authorities concerning the value of certain machines for purchase tax[49] and, more relevantly, to a complaint by a member of the public to the NSPCC concerning alleged child abuse.[50] Yet the courts are also anxious to emphasise that confidentiality is not to become a screen behind which refuge can be taken particularly where the matter is essentially one of private right and not concerned with information necessary to the proper working of the government of the state. Thus in Science Research Council v Nasse (1979) 3 WLR 722 the House of Lords refused public interest immunity to confidential reports on employees applying for promotion or transfer. And in the recent case of Campbell v Thameside Metropolitan Borough Council (1982) 3 WLR 74 disclosure was ordered of documents and reports (including a psychiatrist's report and a teacher's report) on a schoolboy of 11 who attacked one of his teachers. It was held that these documents were of crucial significance in showing the boy's violent disposition and to refuse disclosure would amount to a denial of justice. A balancing act is thus being performed: what will be the outcome of a particular plea of privilege will depend, to some extent as least, on who is the pivot, and the general social and political background of the moment.

NOTES

1. Even though the words are not defamatory they may be actionable in the separate and distinct action for malicious or injurious falsehood. This action is not concerned with injury to reputation. To succeed the plaintiff must prove that the words complained of were untrue, that they were published maliciously and that he has thereby been caused special damage or is exempted from so proving by Section 3 of the Defamation Act 1952.

2 An indictment will lie where either the libel tends to provoke the person defamed to commit a breach of the peace or where it is in the public interest that proceedings should be brought. By s 6 of the Libel Act 1843 it is a defence to show the truth of the defamatory matter and that its publication was for the public benefit. Note also that to support a criminal prosecution it is not essential that publication should have been made to a third person. A criminal prosecution for libel on a dead person can be brought if the libel was intended to injure the living and provoke a breach of the peace: R v Topham (1791) 4 Term Rep 126.

3 Slander will be actionable per se where the words charge the plaintiff which having committed a criminal offence punishable with imprisonment, where they impute that the plaintiff has certain contagious diseases: Bloodworth v Gray (1844) 7 Man and G 344, where they impute unchastity or adultery to any woman or girl: Slander of Women Act 1891 or where they are calculated to disparage the plaintiff in any office profession trade or business held or carried on by him at the time of the publication: s 2 Defamation Act 1952. Special damage may be awarded in respect of any material temporal injury which is either a pecuniary loss or capable of being estimated in money: Roberts v Roberts (1864) 5 B&S 384.

4 See the Defamation Act 1952 s 1 and the Theatres Act 1968 s 4(1).

5 See Report of Faulks Committee (Cmnd 5909) Appendix VI and J.M. Kaye, Libel and Slander - Two tests or One (1975) 91 LQR 524 and an article by Lord Lloyd of Hampstead in Current Legal Problems

(1976) p. 184.

6 The proper and only person to bring the action is the person actually and personally defamed. It therefore follows that an action for libel and slander does not lie in respect of a dead person: Hatchard v Mege (1887) 18 QBD. As for group libel, see below.

7 The Faulks committee recommended the following definition: 'Defamation shall consist of the publication to a third party of a matter which in all the circumstances would be likely to affect a person adversely in the estimation of reasonable people generally.' Cmnd 5909 para 65.

8 Byrne v Deane (1937) 1 KB 818 where it was said 'in my view to say or allege of a man . . . that he has reported certain acts, wrongful in law, to the police, cannot posibly be said to be defamatory of him in the minds of the general public.' Per Slasser L.J; at page 832.

9 s 2 of the Defamation Act 1952 The effect of this provision is to abolish the old requirement of proof of special damage where the defamatory words were not spoken of the plaintiff in the way of his profession or business. See Jones v Jones 1916 2 AC 481 where it was held not slanderous to say of a head master that he was committing adultery with a cleaner of the school.

10 Youssoupoff v Metro-Goldwyn-Mayer Pictures Ltd (1934) 50 TLR 581.

11 E. Hulton v Jones (1910) AC 20. But see also the defence of innocent dissemination s 4 of the Defamation Act 1952.

12 Cassidy v Daily Mirror Newspapers Ltd (1929) 2 KB 331.

13 See note 2 above.

14 Golding v Torch Printing 1949 (4) SALF 150 where it was said that a school master was well known for giving riotous parties. For further illustrations of what is defamatory see Gatley on Libel at para 50 et seq.

15 See note w.

16 Pullman v Hill and Co (1891) 1 QB 524.

17 McPherson v Daniels (1829) 10 B&C 263.

18 Speight v Gosnay (1891) 60 LJQB 231.

19 Knupffer v London Express Newspaper (1944) AC 116.

20 ibid, page 116.

21 ibid, page 124 per Lord Porter.

22 Apart from those discussed, see also: an offer of amends under the Defamation Act 1952 s 4, leave or licence, innocent dissemination and apology and payment into court under Lord Campbell's Acts 1843 and 1845.

23 Subject to the provision of the Rehabilitation of Offenders Act 1974.

24 Bishop v Latimer (1861) 4 LT 775.

25 See the Faulks Committee recommendation at paras 129 and 144.

26 See Halsbury's Laws of England, Volume 28, para 135. Cox v Feeney (1863) 4 f&F13 where it was held that the management of a college is a matter of public interest. In London Artists v Littler (1969) 2QB 375 Lord Denning at page 391 said: 'Whenever a matter is

such as to affect people at large, so that they may be legitimately interested in, or concerned at, what is going on or what may happen to them or others, then it is a matter of public interest on which everyone is entitled to make fair comment.'

27   In South Hetton Coal Co v North-Eastern News Association (1894) 1 QB 133 it was held that the insanitary conditions of a number of cottages owned by a colliery company was a matter of public interest.

28   Fair comment – In an action for libel or slander in respect of words consisting partly of allegations of fact and partly of expressions of opinion, a defence of fair comment shall not fail by reason only that the truth of every allegation of fact is not proved if the expressions of opinion is fair comment having regard to such of the facts alleged or referred to in the words complained of as are proved.' Where the facts are not stated by the commentator but merely indicated by him the common law rule is less strict: Kemsley v Foot 1952 AC 345.

29   Silkin v Beaverbrook Newspapers (1958) 2 A11 ER 516.

30   Campbell v Spottsiwoode (1836) 3 B&S 769.

31   Tadd v Eastwood, Times Law Report 28th May 1983.

32   Apart from the instances examined further, it should be noted that reports of Parliamentary proceedings, extracts from Parliamentary papers and public registers, certain reports published in newspapers or by broadcasting coming within s 7 of the Defamation Act 1952 also enjoy qualified privilege.

33   Stuart v Bell (1891) 2 QB 350

34   Hume v Marshall (1877) 42 JP 136

35   See also s 7 of the Defamation Act 1952 and s 9 of the Act.

36   Ibid.

37   Horrocks v Lowe (1975) AC 135

38   Exemplary damages may be awarded a) where the plaintiff has been injured by oppressive, arbitrary or unconstitutional action by servants of the Government b) where the defendant has deliberately committed a tort with the intention of gaining some advantage which he calculates will outweigh any sum that he may have to pay the plaintiff by way of compensation c) where exemplary damages are expressly authorised by statue. See generally Cassell v Broome (1972) AC 1027 and Rookes v Barnard (1964) AC 1129.

39   See generally Cross on Evidence, 5th Ed, at page 153.

40   A few exceptions exist – see further Cross on Evidence, ibid.

41   Whenever the term 'witness' is used it also includes parties to the proceedings, though there are certain respects in which the position of a party differs from that of an ordinary witness.

42   See Cross, bid, page 273.

43   D v NSPCC (1978) AC 171 where it was held that the public interest concerned was the welfare of the children: hence the true analogy was with the confidentiality recognised by the courts in civil proceedings in the case of names of police informers. See also Campbell v Thameside MBC (1982) 3 WLR 74.

44   See Cross ibid at page 280 and Statutory Restrictions on the Privilege against Self-incrimination by J.D. Heydon 87 LQR 214.

45   Wheeler v Le Marchand (1881) 17 Ch D 675.

46   Cross, ibid, page 295.   See also British Steel Corporation v Granada Television (1980) 3 WLR 774, where the rule was re-affirmed that journalists have no immunity based on public interest against disclosure of their sources of information when such disclosure is necessary in the interests of justice.

47   See, for general principle, Duncan v Cammell Laird (1942) AC 624 at 636.

48   Marks v Beyfous (1890) 25 QBD 494

49   Alfred Crompton Amusement Machines v Commissioner for Customs and Excise (1974) AC 405.

50   D V NSPCC, infra.

CONTRIBUTORS

RICHARD PRING is Professor of Education at the University of Exeter.

JOHN ELLIOTT is Tutor at the Cambridge Institute of Education.

MICHAEL ERAUT is Reader in Education at the University of Sussex.

CLEM ADELMAN is Research Co-ordinator at Bulmershe College of Higher Education.

HELEN SIMONS is Lecturer in Curriculum Studies at the London Institute of Education.

IAN JAMIESON has recently completed an evaluation of the Schools Council Industry project.

LAWRENCE STENHOUSE was lately, Director of the Centre for Applied Research in Education, University of East Anglia.

ANN McALLISTER is a Barrister.